A Relational Model of Public Discourse

Contemporary democratic discourses are frequently, though not exclusively, characterized by an attitude of 'pro and con' where the aim is to persuade others, a jury or an audience, of what is right and what is wrong. Challenging such procedures, this book teases out an alternative model of public discourse that is based in collaboration and deliberation. The African philosophy of *ubuntu* offers valuable insights in this regard as it implies relational notions of power that contrast and complement individualist facets. It provides the space to think and speak in ways that support harmonious and cohesive societal structures and practices. The book's model of communication rests on the premise that the various interests of individuals and groups, while richly diverse, can be conceived of as profoundly bound-up rather than incompatible. In this way communication enables broader lines of action and a wider scope for achieving diversity and common ground.

Leyla Tavernaro-Haidarian is a media professional and communication specialist researching in the areas of communication, public discourse, education and governance at the University of Johannesburg, South Africa.

Routledge Focus on Communication Studies

A Relational Model of Public Discourse
The African Philosophy of *Ubuntu*
Leyla Tavernaro-Haidarian

A Relational Model of Public Discourse

The African Philosophy of *Ubuntu*

Leyla Tavernaro-Haidarian

Routledge
Taylor & Francis Group

LONDON AND NEW YORK

First published 2018
by Routledge

2 Park Square, Milton Park, Abingdon, Oxfordshire OX14 4RN
52 Vanderbilt Avenue, New York, NY 10017

Routledge is an imprint of the Taylor & Francis Group, an informa business

First issued in paperback 2019

Library of Congress Cataloging-in-Publication Data
A catalog record for this book has been requested

ISBN: 978-0-8153-6366-8 (hbk)
ISBN: 978-0-367-89268-5 (pbk)

Typeset in Times New Roman
by Apex CoVantage, LLC

Contents

Preface

Living in South Africa and learning about the philosophy of *ubuntu* has been a privilege. *Ubuntu*, which roughly translates as 'I am because we are', is an idea, a notion and a way of life that emerges in one's day-to-day interactions with people and which is best experienced rather than talked of. Yet my intention here has been to use my very words to introduce and explore this philosophy in order that hearts are moved and souls are stirred. And while many scholars sanitize *ubuntu* from its spiritual origins, it is impossible to deny its transcendent dimensions, which are somewhat lost in the academic exercise that is this book. It is my hope, however, that readers identify with 'I am because we are', with the unifying, the cohesive, the harmonious and that it sparks some thought as to its place in the current state of our world.

This idea of *ubuntu* has carried South Africa through some of its darkest chapters of institutionalized racism and into the break of dawn. And though the work is certainly not over and nobody anywhere can afford to relax in the face of the vast challenges and inequalities that still exist we can learn from those strategies that have worked and those that clearly continue not to. In this book I honor that which has worked—driving darkness out with light—and I invite the reader to consider an approach to communication and public discourse that seeks to bring people of various backgrounds together in their collective pursuit of truth. This approach is premised on our oneness as a human family and considers our affairs as profoundly relational and bound-up. It encourages us to contextualize our experiences and views and to look toward that which we can build together rather than that which we've been conditioned to blindly defend.

Unfortunately, this is not always easy. The idea of unity has often been hijacked by those who feel far from bound-up with their fellow human beings and who universalize, instead, their own narratives and experiences.

But this does not make the principles of oneness and cohesion any less attractive, relevant or pressing. We simply have to transcend this misappropriation and reclaim diversity by striving with pure intent.

It is of course possible to dismiss such an effort as entirely idealistic and unrealistic, yet it is also convenient to do so. Relegating social cohesion and cooperation to the realm of something that is utopian means that we do not have to exert effort or strain to make a difference in the world around us. So I offer this book as an invitation to strive and to make a change.

In the words of my beloved Bahá'u'lláh (1817–1892):

> The wellbeing of mankind, its peace and security are unattainable unless and until its unity is firmly established.

Leyla Tavernaro-Haidarian, PhD

Introduction

One of the remarkable features of present-day discourses is their tendency to manifest as wars of words, which in some cases "play as significant a role as wars of weapons" (Ramsbotham, 2010:xi). These tendencies extend far beyond political debates and can be evidenced in many mass-mediated contexts, such as in the realm of reality television for example. As a producer I have often seen commercial media organizations choose and cultivate those aspects of a story that lend themselves to conflict, drama and spectacle and write off collaborative programming ideas as 'too earnest' for their liking. Instead, contestants battle it out in the kitchen, on an island or in the gym. In the studio, a group of entrepreneurs compete for an investment and talk show hosts prompt their guests to spill the beans and make shocking and controversial confessions regarding their personal lives. And while it is easy to write off these strategies as entertaining and harmless, my project here is to show that many of the assumptions implicit in them are problematic and that they can inhibit collaboration and social justice where alternatives are more effective. Specifically, I introduce the African philosophy of *ubuntu* and discuss what it teaches us about how we should relate to one another and how we could structure public discourses more effectively.

One approach that is often thought to be effective, natural and inevitable is to shape discourses as conflicts of interest that are enmeshed in postures of offense and defense. This is combined with a persuasive approach to rhetoric, where the aim is to win or persuade an opponent (see Karlberg, 2004; Tannen, 1998). Discussions around parenting are a case in point. Many popular talk show programs will frame parenting matters in exclusionary or binary ways between 'stay-at-home moms' and 'working moms' as though there were an intrinsic conflict of interest between child-care and equality (see Urban, 2009). In a case like this, issues such as personal circumstance, culture, religion, the role of fathers, employers, government, affordable child-care or 'building the right village' are completely obscured. As is the possibility that stay-at-home moms and working moms might actually be the same people.

This type of 'argument culture' (Tannen, 1998) frequently emerges in broadly libertarian, free press media systems (McQuail, 2010) and can be related to the rise of Western liberal thought, which regards society as a sphere of scarce resources and where people vie to realize their divergent interests (Karlberg, 2012:22). It informs large portions of the philosophical fabric of contemporary societies (Moulton, 1983; Trompkins, 1988), including the way we argue and frame debates in academia, in court or in politics and it significantly contrasts the more relational approaches found in other ethical traditions. In Chinese thought, for example,

> Aesthetic analogies with music, food and dance are frequently invoked to explain what harmony is. [. . .] It is a matter of different elements coming together, where differences are not merely respected, but also integrated in such a way that the best of them is brought out and something new is created.
>
> (Metz, 2014:150)

Though this idea may have been abused historically, the foundational assumptions inherent in this philosophy and in many others from Thailand, Japan and elsewhere in Asia emphasize harmony rather than conflict and significantly contrast the assumptions inherent in argument culture.

While of course no genre, program or forum is entirely and exclusively made up of argument culture, the broadly argumentative strategies that can be traced throughout the spectrum of public discourse are not without value and have certainly had their merits. They can, for example, provide a platform and visibility for underrepresented segments of society as they do in conflict-driven talk shows or tabloids. Here Wasserman (2013:75–76) suggests that, despite their sensationalism, tabloids have often provided a democratically inclusive and participatory forum for the public. So the social, cultural and political issues that arise through agonistic strategies can be significant. They have also contributed to emancipating societies from previously authoritarian or oppressive systems and their excesses of power (Karlberg, 2012:22). Such excesses have been kept in check by democracies organizing society as a contest of ideas and by creating an environment of accountability through strategies of contestation and argumentation.

Yet it is also possible to identify limitations to this approach. Deutsch (2000:28), for example, suggests that competitive debate can be counterproductive because,

> there is usually a winner and a loser. The party judged to have 'the best' ideas, skills, knowledge, and so on, typically wins while the other, who is judged to be less good, loses. Competition evaluates and ranks people based on their capacity for a particular task, rather than integrating various contributions.

He motivates moving beyond narrow competitiveness and toward the cultivation of discourses, which seek "a solution that integrates the best thoughts that emerge during the discussion, no matter who articulates them" (Deutsch, 2006:28). In this way a "clash of differing opinions" ('Abdu'l-Bahá, 1978:87) can emerge, which is unrestrained by adversarial strategies. Such strategies tend to exclude gentler, less aggressive voices and are often reductionist, failing to address the full complexity of the issues they explore and obscuring common ground where it may indeed exist (Karlberg, 1997). Large segments of society, for example, identify with the views of multiple political parties but having to vote for one or the other limits this complexity and so many citizens disengage from the political process altogether.

From time to time, however, common ground does emerge even in the most conflictual of set-ups. I have often witnessed adversaries suddenly agreeing, game-show contestants spontaneously cooperating. This indicates that, despite formal attempts to draw out conflict in many situations, people are also prone to collaborate and cooperate. It would then be compelling to explore what outcomes deliberately cooperative and participatory strategies of public discourse could yield, which assume interconnectivity as their underlying realism. In the above-mentioned case, for example, stay-at-home moms and working moms could well agree (together with other community members) on the principles and strategies they believe would create nurturing and stimulating environments for their children to grow up in. For such discourses relational approaches could be more enabling.

Likewise, for many societies pursuing post-colonial ways of thinking, talking and doing, alternatives are worth considering. For them, Western liberal strategies might not be the most authentic approach. As Rao and Wasserman (2007:33) propose, "the normative frameworks of liberal democracy cannot be unproblematically applied to contexts outside of the West". In many nations, such as South Africa or India for example, colonialism has brought with it values, systems and discourses that are incompatible with the realities they find themselves in. For such societies and for those acutely aware of the exigencies of our interconnected age, it is vital that more relevant and relational models of public discourse are explored and developed.

However, reimagining our normative assumptions requires an effort to look toward and learn from other cultures and contexts and to integrate these insights into an evolving framework for conceptualizing social organization. This is what people such as President Nelson Mandela and Archbishop Desmond Tutu did when they began articulating the idea of a diverse and unified reality for a racially divided South Africa before this was in any way operational (see Salazar, 2002). Such notions can be extended to a wider context, where the engagement with multiple normative frameworks from many parts of the world may lead to cross-pollination and the development and innovation of approaches in such areas as communication, governance, economics and justice. There is a lot to be learned from the world's ethico-cultural repository and from places like South Africa, which, in the aftermath of White supremacy, or *apartheid*, manifested a reconciliatory approach to justice rather than a retributive one. I would also imagine that a similarly relational approach to communication would be more instrumental for community/unity building than an adversarial one.

In South Africa, for example, notions such as "truth, justice and authority" are "based on collective consciousness", ethical decision-making is grounded in the values of the community and community is closely linked to the individual (Rao & Wasserman, 2007:40). Rediscovering and exploring such relational values becomes "part of the renegotiation of cultural identities" and "can be seen as a post-colonial process" (ibid.) that reimagines and re-evaluates the status quo. It requires us to ask what kind of communication and which ethico-cultural frameworks will best suit today's highly diverse yet wholly interdependent (and to a large extent post-colonial) societies around the world?

One strategy has been to look at how various normative theories of democracy can inform and evolve approaches to media and communication (see Baker, 2007; Christians et al., 2009; Strömbäck, 2006). In this context, Bitzer (2009) suggests that deliberative democracy is highly relevant to societies everywhere. Against the interest-based conception of democracy, which is inspired if not beholden by economics, proponents of deliberative democracy are looking for spaces that promote popular participation and public deliberation and where citizens can share commonalities and respect differences (see Callan, 1997; Cooke, 2000; Habermas, 1996; Matyni, 2009). But although such models of democracy are frequently thought of as challenging the dominant Western liberal paradigm in media and communication studies they have now become a major reference point in their own right (Karpinnen, 2013:n.p.) and, as I suggest later on, mostly derive from the same realism that informs the Western liberal one. So it is amid calls to evolve from the Habermasian idea of the public sphere (see Karpinnen, 2013) that efforts to consider alternatives become important. With that in mind, my book contributes to the generation and development of such a framework. Though wholly non-exhaustive in its scope, it engages with yet distinguishes itself from deliberative democracy and many other expressions of mutualism found in the global North.

It particular, it draws on the deep sense of relationalism that informed South Africa's post-*apartheid* reconciliatory stance and much of its public discourse. This was largely characterized by "unifying words and symbols" and was "a remarkable rhetorical accomplishment, overcoming the deep wounds of class and race, forging a multicultural nation out of the former oppressed and oppressors" Bazerman (2002:xiii). A significant cultural value that can be associated with this process is *ubuntu*. The African moral theory of *ubuntu*, commonly understood as 'I am because we are' (Mkhize, 2008:40; Mnyaka & Motlhabi, 2005:218; Tutu, 1999:35), is chiefly collaborative in nature and has been "articulated as one of the key philosophies underpinning South African governance and service delivery" (see Rodny-Gumede, 2015a:110). *Ubuntu* is a value that is both descriptive of the way we are inherently bound together and prescriptive for how one is to realize one's true self specifically in terms of communal, harmonious or cohesive relationships with others (Metz, 2011; Metz & Gaie, 2010; Mnyaka & Motlhabi, 2005). It constitutes a form of communal engagement where diversity flourishes and it favors relational approaches to governance and communication.

Inspired by this, several scholars have already begun exploring the sub-Saharan notion of *ubuntu* as a basis for the media to serve as a forum for thoughtful and constructive processes of democratic deliberation (see Blankenberg, 1999; Christians, 2000, 2004; Ess, 2013; Fourie, 2011; Metz, 2015; Rodny-Gumede, 2015b; Rao & Wasserman, 2007; Tomaselli, 2011; Wasserman, 2013). However, most of what is written on *ubuntu* in relation to the media remains focused on journalism ethics. As with the literature on deliberative democracy, it also does not explicitly invite a shift from reactive or conflictual ways of conceiving the world to more harmonious ones. With this book, on the other hand, I explore the more practical dimensions of *ubuntu*-based communication and consider the consequences of an explicitly relational realism, derived from its cohesive conceptions of power.

Such conceptions, however, are not those that "simplistically yearn for pristinely pure social orders characterized by harmony" (Chasi, 2014a:300). As Chasi (ibid.) critically notes, while some scholars take as their departure point a view that the world is in fact harmonious or that it could be harmonious, *ubuntu* remains relevant even if one were to assume that it is indeed a violent place. Yet it is also possible to consider, as I do, that the world is neither fundamentally harmonious nor fundamentally violent but rather that human beings are potentially capable of both expressions. And since we have ample experience with conflictual strategies of social organization, it is attractive to experiment with deliberately harmonious ones to see what fruits those might yield.

In this context, I am interested in exploring how a practically applicable model of public discourse based in *ubuntu*'s assumptions of harmony and complementarity could extend to many forms of media and discourse and how this might be relevant for the broader field of communication everywhere. Toward this end, I bring into clearer focus elements of a participatory model of public discourse where "every person is regarded as a foundation of knowledge that has valuable things to contribute to society as a whole" (Blankenberg, 1999:51). I call this approach 'deliberation culture' rather than 'argument culture' and offer it as a contribution to the existing literature of *ubuntu*-based ethics and to the field of communication more generally.

At first and because of the post-colonial processes associated with both, the term 'deliberation culture' may be confused and associated too closely with the concept of deliberative democracy. There are, of course, diverse views about the exact definition of deliberative democracy and insofar as it facilitates a dialogical, reflexive and "unconstrained exchange of viewpoints, involves practical reasoning and potentially leads to a transformation of preferences" (Cooke, 2000:948) those associations make sense. Yet 'deliberative' also invokes echoes of Habermas (2006) on the one hand and Mouffe (1999) on the other, the latter who critically proposes that deliberation actually suggests a violent process based in conflictual ways of perceiving the world. This is not the case with deliberation culture. Therefore, it should not be tied too much to these definitions. The concept of deliberation culture is only loosely situated within the spectrum of deliberative democracy and is completely distinct. With it I offer an alternative, as it were, to Mouffe's (1999) 'agonistic pluralism' and more specifically an alternative to Tannen's (1998) argument culture in the form of a process that is deeply relational, harmonious and indeed 'consultative' (see Kolstoe, 1990).

The term 'deliberation culture' is inspired by the cohesive attitude of *ubuntu* and the way traditional African democracy functions as a sometimes lengthy deliberation (see De Liefde, 2005) known as an *indaba, pungwe* or *lekgotla*, where members of the community are afforded an equal opportunity to share their thoughts until a form of agreement, consensus or cohesion is reached (see Blankenberg, 1999; Louw, 2010). I address this deliberative attitude in more detail in the following chapters. It can be summed up in words like *simunye* ('we are one') or *sawubona* ('I see you'), which assume harmony rather than conflict.

Thus, while deliberative democracy may ensure diversity through "confrontation" (Bitzer, 2009), through "distress and belligerence" (Callan, 1997), deliberation culture achieves this through exploration and invitation. It extends beyond the aim of coexistence (as expressed in deliberative democracy) and explicitly works toward harmonious and bound-up outcomes. This highlights the difference between intention and modality. The intention of a debate, for example, may very well be reconciliatory rather than divisive yet it can still employ a reactive or argumentative mode of communication in the process. Abrahamson's (2004) model of 'confrontative dialogue' (which I refer to in my concluding chapter) is a compelling example of this. It seeks to address power inequalities and has been applied to numerous contexts that aim to transcend ideological polarization. The question, however, is whether facilitating such egalitarian intentions in a deliberately cohesive manner may not be even more effective in bringing together various groups and individuals. In this context, I think of *ubuntu* as being able to inspire such relational and harmonious approaches to communication, societal thought and practice.

However, the cohesive attitude of *ubuntu* is not to be confused with collectivist or corporatist notions that can lead to false acquiescence or the abuse of power, as in some cultural instances (see Ramsbotham, 2010:5). Rather it is to be read in terms of harmonious interactions between diverse individuals, where the individual is treated "as special in virtue of her capacity to enter into relationships of identity and solidarity" (Metz, 2015:78). As such I consider *ubuntu* primarily as an ideal theory rather than in its historic or anthropological sense, although I make references to historic moments where it has played out in this ideal sense. *Ubuntu* has been used to promote both the morally desirable as well as the questionable (see Chasi, 2014b) and because it can be taken up in unwanted and essentialist ways (see Tomaselli, 2009), it is vital to balance this "vaguely African" philosophy with the exigencies of "the here and now" (Blankenberg, 1999:43) and to "constantly reinvent" it (Chasi, 2014b:496). *Ubuntu* exists alongside other contradictory euphemisms and proverbs in sub-Saharan Africa and so I elaborate on it as an ongoing and dynamic concept in order to work with a non-essentialist, contemporary conception that can serve as a compelling possible "foundation for public morality" (Metz, 2011:559) and can help fulfill "our deepest moral obligation of entering more and more deeply into community with others" (Shutte, 2001:30).

The relevance of *ubuntu* in shaping public discourses is underscored by the literature that explores how global ethical matters might be approached differently if values such as *ubuntu* were taken seriously in spheres such as politics, foreign relations or criminal justice (see Metz, 2014). Bujo (1997), Gyekye (1997), Metz (2014) and Wiredu (1998), for example, propose that *ubuntu*'s concern for harmony is conducive to non-competitive forms of decision-making where unanimous, consensus-oriented rather than majoritarian agreement is considered ideal and a non-party polity is desirable. Such relational approaches to governance and international affairs "tell against [. . .] the notion of isolationism, avoiding other countries' problems altogether" as there is "some positive obligation to aid others as a key way to manifest a harmonious relationship" (Metz, 2014:152). Together with the reconciliatory approach to justice derived from *ubuntu*, where reform and restoration constitute key features, these examples indicate that changing the ethico-cultural approaches to our dominant discourses can significantly impact related social practices.

My overall objective with this book, then, is to articulate what *ubuntu* has to offer in the form of a relational approach to public discourse. This can be further refined and cross-pollinated with other strategies from around the world. Importantly, my intention is not to juxtapose two cultural models (i.e. 'Western' versus 'African') in some sort of clash or duel. Rather, the idea is to acknowledge and discuss the strengths and weaknesses of one salient model and to then suggest an alternative with contrasting underpinnings. This alternative is based in the ideas associated with *ubuntu* yet also engages with and draws on other theories from the global North. As such, it is integrative and outward looking. My underlying objectives are to question the hegemony of adversarial strategies in communication; to analyze the realism that informs them and to offer a compelling alternative rooted in the relational, harmonious and cohesive understandings of power associated with *ubuntu*.

I do this by discussing the broader cultural and historical context of contemporary discourses (see Fairclough, 1989; Van Dijk, 2001) and more specifically the discursive strategies related to argument culture. I then explore how the key features of argument culture are informed by conflictual understandings of power and how they might manifest differently if they were informed by relational ones. I consider these features as analytical constructs that may not always correspond fully with reality but rather serve to organize inquiry and reshape praxis. I also draw on insight stimulating examples from the media and discuss these against some of the pertinent literature on discourse, culture, power and *ubuntu* in order to regulate my perspectives and experiences. I then articulate a relational model of public discourse based in *ubuntu*. I offer this as a form of discourse engagement or discourse expansion as I build on the theories I engage with. My chapters unfold as follows:

In the first chapter, I introduce key concepts relating to discourse and culture. I outline how discourses are influenced by their wider ethico-cultural context and how they can evolve. I submit that we largely live in a 'culture of contest' (Karlberg, 2004), where individualism is often favored and contests are assumed to be normal and necessary models of social organization. As a normative alternative, I explore the African philosophy of *ubuntu*. *Ubuntu* provides a relational and harmonious realism from within which discourses can be reshaped.

In Chapter 2, I discuss how *ubuntu* expands the way we conceive of power. I briefly outline predominant and alternative conceptions of power from the global North and explain how these tie in with their greater ethico-cultural context. I then show how conceptions of power implicit in *ubuntu* differ by assuming that human affairs are profoundly bound-up rather than divergent. I describe how *ubuntu* foregrounds immaterial aspects of power rooted in force rather than substance and what this means for the ways in which we can relate and organize.

Next, I turn to the structural properties of discourse in Chapter 3. I begin by deconstructing the constituent variables of 'argument culture' (Tannen, 1998), which include a narrow, often binary framing of issues and a chiefly persuasive approach to rhetoric. I then discuss how identity is formed and mediation is facilitated in reactionary and opposing ways by referring to related theories and providing a critical discourse analysis of examples from the media.

By drawing on and contrasting the constituent elements of argument culture, I then begin the project of synthesizing an alternative concept of communication in Chapter 4. What I term 'deliberation culture' is rooted in *ubuntu* and is deeply relational. It constitutes a harmonious and collaborative model of inquiry that encourages relativity and flexibility and stimulates diversity and participation. It entails an open-ended way of framing, a chiefly exploratory posture, a 'we' identity that promotes diversity and mediation that is facilitatory.

In the concluding chapter, I summarize my ideas and analyses and consider the broader applications and implications of this model in various settings. I reflect on the wider socio-cultural conditions that may limit its efficacy and suggest that deliberation culture is one of many vital and ongoing efforts to evolve democratic processes.

With this project I hope to give mutualistic approaches to communication and governance more visibility and to show that there are many values beyond those inherited through colonialism that can and must contribute to the shaping of our world. Elements of deliberation culture already exist and spontaneously appear in many contexts in southern Africa and beyond. Its strategies emerge in broader mediated contexts and through this book I bring them together into a coherent concept that can be applied where public matters are negotiated in collaborative ways, where a plurality and multiplicity of voices is cherished and consensus is sought.

References

'Abdu'l-Bahá (1978). *Selections from the Writings of 'Abdu'l-Bahá.* Haifa: Baha'i World Center.

Abrahamson, H. (2004). The Role of Dialogue in Confronting Power, Paper presented to the Department of Peace and Development Studies, January 2004, Gothenburg, Sweden.

Baker, E.C. (2007). *Media Concentration and Democracy.* New York: Cambridge University Press.

Bazerman, C. (2002). Foreword. In Salazar, P.J. (ed). *An African Athens: Rhetoric and the Shaping of Democracy in South Africa.* Mahwah/London: Lawrence Erlbaum.

Bitzer, E. (2009). *Higher Education in South Africa: A Scholarly Look behind the Scenes.* Stellenbosch: Sun Media.

Blankenberg, N. (1999). In Search of Real Freedom: Ubuntu and the Media. *Critical Arts,* 12(2):42–65.

Bujo, B. (1997). *The Ethical Dimension of Community.* Nairobi: Paulines Publications Africa.

Callan, E. (1997). *Creating Citizens: Political Education and Liberal Democracy.* Oxford: Oxford University Press.

Chasi, C. (2014a). Violent Communication Is Not Alien to Ubuntu: Nothing Human Is Alien to Africans. *Communicatio: South African Journal for Communication Theory and Research,* 40(4):287–304.

Chasi, C. (2014b). Ubuntu and Freedom of Expression. *Ethics & Behavior*, 24(6): 495–509.

Christians, C.G. (2000). Social Dialogue and Media Ethics. *Ethical Perspectives*, 7(2–3):182.

Christians, C.G. (2004). Ubuntu and Communitarianism in Media Ethics. *Ecquid Novi*, 25(2):235–256.

Christians, C.G., Glasser, T.H., McQuail, D., Nordenstreng, K. & White, R.A. (2009). *Normative Theories of the Media*. Urbana/Chicago: University of Illinois Press.

Cooke, M. (2000). Five Arguments for Deliberative Democracy. *Political Studies Association*, 48(1):947–969.

De Liefde, W.H.J. (2005). *Lekgotla: The Art of Leadership through Dialogue*. Cape Town: Jacana.

Deutsch, M. (2006). Cooperation and Competition. In Deutsch, M. & Coleman, P. (eds). *The Handbook of Conflict Resolution: Theory and Practice*: 21–40, San Francisco: Jossey-Bass.

Ess, C. (2013). *Digital Media Ethics*. Oxford: Polity Press.

Fairclough, N. (1989). *Language and Power*. London: Longman.

Fourie, P. (2011). Normative Media Theory in a Changed Media Landscape and Globalized Society. In Hyde-Clarke, N. (ed). *Communication and Media Ethics in South Africa*: 25–45, Cape Town: Juta.

Gyekye, K. (1997). *Tradition and Modernity: Philosophical Reflections on the African Experience*. New York: Oxford University Press.

Habermas, J. (1996). *Between Facts and Norms*. Cambridge: MIT.

Habermas, J. (2006). *The Divided West*. Cambridge: Polity Press.

Karlberg, M. (1997). News and Conflict: How Adversarial News Frames Limit Public Understanding of Environmental Issues. *Alternatives Journal*, 23(1):33–48.

Karlberg, M. (2004). *Beyond the Culture of Contest*. Oxford: George Ronald.

Karlberg, M. (2012). Reframing Public Discourses for Peace and Justice. In Korostelina, K. (ed). *Forming a Culture of Peace: Reframing Narratives of Intergroup Relations, Equity and Justice*: 15–42, London: Palgrave Macmillan.

Karpinnen, K. (2013). Uses of Democratic Theory in Media and Communication Studies, *Observatorio*, 7(3):n.p.

Kolstoe, J.E. (1990). *Consultation: A Universal Lamp of Guidance*. Oxford: George Ronald.

Louw, D.J. (2010). Power Sharing and the Challenge of Ubuntu Ethics, Paper presented at the Forum for Religious Dialogue Symposium of the Research Institute for Theology and Religion at the University of South Africa, January 2010, Pretoria, South Africa.

Matyni, E. (2009). *Performative Democracy*. Boulder: Paradigm.

McQuail, D. (2010). *Mass Communication Theory*. University of Amsterdam: Sage.

Metz, T. (2011). Ubuntu as a Moral Theory and Human Rights in South Africa. *African Human Rights Law Journal*, 11(1):532–559.

Metz, T. (2014). Harmonizing Global Ethics in the Future: A Proposal to Add South and East to West. *Journal of Global Ethics*, 10(2):146–155.

Metz, T. (2015). African Ethics and Journalism Ethics: News and Opinion in Light of Ubuntu. *Journal of Media Ethics: Exploring Questions of Media Morality*, 30(2):74–90.

Metz, T. & Gaie, J. (2010). The African Ethic of Ubuntu/Botho: Implications for Research on Morality. *Journal of Moral Education*, 39(1):273–290.

Mkhize, N. (2008). Ubuntu and Harmony: An African Approach to Morality and Ethics. In Nicolson, R. (ed). *Persons in Community: African Ethics in a Global Culture*: 35–44, Pietermaritzburg: University of KwaZulu-Natal Press.

Mnyaka, M. & Motlhabi, M. (2005). The African Concept of Ubuntu/Botho and Its Socio-Moral Significance. *Black Theology*, 3(1):215–237.

Mouffe, C. (1999). Deliberative Democracy or Agonistic Pluralism? *Social Research*, 66(3):745–758.

Moulton, J. (1983). A Paradigm of Philosophy: The Adversary Method. In Harding, S. & Hintikka, M. (eds). *Discovering Reality: Feminist Perspectives on Epistemology, Metaphysics, Methodology, and Philosophy of Science*. New York: Springer.

Ramsbotham, O. (2010). *Transforming Violent Conflict: Radical Disagreement, Dialogue and Survival*. London: Routledge.

Rao, S. & Wasserman, H. (2007). Global Media Ethics Revisited: A Postcolonial Critique. *Global Media and Communication*, 3(1):29–50.

Rodny-Gumede, Y. (2015a). An Assessment of the Public Interest and Ideas of the Public in South Africa and the Adoption of Ubuntu Journalism. *Journal of Mass Media Ethics*, 30(2):109–124.

Rodny-Gumede, Y. (2015b). Coverage of Marikana: War and Conflict and the Case for Peace (Journalism). *Social Dynamics*, 41(2):359–374.

Salazar, P.J. (2002). *An African Athens: Rhetoric and the Shaping of Democracy in South Africa*. Mahwah/London: Lawrence Erlbaum.

Shutte, A. (2001). *Ubuntu: An Ethic for the New South Africa*. Cape Town: Cluster Publications.

Strömbäck, J. (2006). In Search of a Standard: Four Models of Democracy and Their Normative Implications for Journalism. *Journalism Studies*, 6(3):331–345.

Tannen, D. (1998). *The Argument Culture*. New York: Random House.

Tomaselli, K.G. (2009). (Afri)ethics, Communitarianism and Libertarianism. *International Communication Gazette*, 71(7):577–594.

Tomaselli, K.G. (2011). (Afri)ethics, Communitarianism and the Public Sphere. In Hyde-Clarke, N. (ed). *Communication and Media Ethics in South Africa*. Cape Town: Juta.

Trompkins, J. (1988). Fighting Words: Unlearning to Write the Critical Essay. *The Georgia Review*, 42:585–590.

Tutu, D. (1999). *No Future without Forgiveness*. New York: Random House.

Urban, A. (2009). Dr. Phil Stay-at-Home Mom vs. Working Mom Show, PhD in Parenting, 14 October 2009, www.phdinparenting.com/blog/2009/10/14/dr-phil-stay-at-home-mom-vs-working-mom-show.html, Accessed 7 August 2017.

Van Dijk, T. (2001). Critical Discourse Analysis. In Schiffrin, D., Tannen, D. & Hamilton, H. (eds). *The Handbook of Discourse Analysis*. Oxford: Blackwell.

Wasserman, H. (2013). Journalism in a New Democracy: The Ethics of Listening. *Communicatio: South African Journal for Communication Theory and Research*, 39(1):67–84.

Wiredu, K. (1998). Democracy and Consensus in African Traditional Politics: A Plea for a Non-Party Polity. In Coetzee, P.H. & Roux, A.P.J. (eds). *Philosophy from Africa*: 374–382, Johannesburg: International Thomson.

1 Discourse, Culture and *Ubuntu*

In light of some of the more extreme manifestations of contemporary discourses characterized by conflict and contention it becomes useful to ask in what ways discourses can be reshaped, elevated and evolved to promote shared ends. In other words what strategies and values we could cultivate that foreground collaboration and background conflict. With that in mind, I begin this chapter by sketching out how discourses can be conceptualized and why some should be reconsidered. This is followed by a brief overview of how ethico-cultural values play a role in shaping and reshaping them. I specifically highlight the concept of 'normative adversarialism' (Karlberg, 2004) as a context or realism that frames many contemporary discourses, discuss some of the reasons it limits us and finally offer the African philosophy of *ubuntu* as a compelling normative alternative.

Discourses unfold everywhere and all the time. They take shape not only in spoken or written form, on television or in the news, but also through the values expressed in photos and billboards, in fashion and sports. According to Fairclough and Wodak (1997:258), discourses can be understood as a "form of 'social practice'", implying "a dialectical relationship between a particular discursive event and the situation(s), institution(s) and social structure(s), which frame it". In other words, discourses are the way we think about concepts and how we express our thoughts in relation to those concepts. They are shaped by and in turn shape the greater socio-cultural context around them (see also Foucault, 1972, 1980; Phillips & Hardy, 2002). So what we say and how we say it does not only describe or reflect the world around us, it also determines it. We project meaning onto things and those meanings affect the way we see them (Fairclough & Wodak, 1997:258). Discourses are not static or fixed but are constantly evolving as we share ideas and change our values. Therefore, a discourse is "constitutive both in the sense that it helps to sustain and reproduce the social status quo, and in the sense that it contributes to transforming it" (Fairclough & Wodak, 1997:258).

Transformation becomes important when we make limiting assumptions about the nature of an issue. In South Africa, for example, discourses around decolonization have been framed both in terms of 'dismantling' strategies (see Booysen, 2016) and 'reshaping' or 'rethinking' strategies (see Isaacs De Vega, 2017). The first frame can be associated with a student movement that demanded access to education and a change in institutional culture. It was accompanied by phrases and hashtags such as 'Fees Must Fall' and 'Rhodes Must Fall' (Booysen, 2016) and its resulting lines of action were chiefly characterized by protests, hostage taking, boycotting, barricading, the throwing of petrol bombs and bricks, the burning of books and other reactive strategies (see Metz, 2016:293). While it achieved much in terms of bring-ing to the fore the pressing inequalities that many South African students face today, framing decolonization as 'dismantling', 'resistance' or 'protest' strategies can only go so far in achieving social transformation. At best, it offers the option of passive resistance, civil disobedience, mass sit-ins and teach-ins or petitions and negotiations (Metz, 2016:298). However, when considering decolonization as a process of 'reshaping' or 'rethinking', other options become available. These include so-called 're-curriculation' efforts that reshape university curricula not only in terms of their content but also in terms of their wider institutional processes. Students, scholars and other stakeholders pour their energies into the development of new paradigms for transforming and delivering higher education. In this way, constructive inno-vations can occur that 'enlarge', 'incorporate', 'include' and 'expand' (see Isaacs De Vega, 2017) as regards ways of being, knowing, doing, student voices and core changes to the institutional eco-system. In other words, how we conceive of the project determines what we can achieve.

Other examples of limiting discourses include divisive or essentialist ways of thinking about race, culture, religion or gender. In fact, a term such as 'race' may carry assumptions about an inherent rather than socially con-structed division of the human family into categories and is created entirely through naturalized ways of thinking and talking. In this way discourses may also be un/intentionally aligned with the perceptions and realities of a privileged few and in particular with those in positions of authority. Jour-nalists, for example, frequently side with elites (political, economic or mili-tary), making their positions seem natural and inevitable. This may "take place unintentionally as a result of established journalistic routines and practices" (Wasserman, 2013:69). Yet when the press is aligned with those who have disproportionate access to the means of cultural production, the established maps of meaning that exist in society are strengthened (ibid.:68) and those who are sidelined by them remain so.

One way to transform such discourses is to clarify and question some of the deeper assumptions that inform them and to unveil and reconsider the power relationships at work (see Derrida, 1978). These can be thought of in terms of their larger cultural and ethical context or realism. Of course cultures are not static and do not exist in silos. Since the beginning of time cultures have evolved and cross-pollinated, be it through force or through voluntary exchanges. They reflect the developmental stages of societies and contain many currents, crosscurrents and sub-currents of attitudes, ideas and behaviors. For example, not all aspects of life in the global North are individualistic or adversarial. There are many expressions of collaboration, symbiosis and mutualism, which emerge from such fields as development studies, feminism, ecology, international law, journalism, mediation and peace studies (see Karlberg, 2004).

According to Karlberg (2004), however, these efforts are often constricted by or subordinated to a larger realism that is 'normative adversarialism', where the unconscious assumption is that human affairs are mutually exclusive and a contest for power is seen as the best way to organize. From within this realism, economics, governance, justice and related social institutions and practices are mainly negotiated in competitive and conflictual terms. This does not always pan out as brash competitiveness or cutthroat competition. It can also unfold in courteous and civil ways. Adversarialism simply refers to a 'culture of contest' (ibid.) and is descriptive of a particular and naturalized style of social organization that can indeed be respectful and dignified. However, it does exercise some considerable hegemony over the way alternative paradigms are perceived. Harmonious, cohesive and relational values often seem naïve from within its realism (see Karlberg, 2004). This explains the prevalence of 'argument culture' (Tannen, 1998), which can be witnessed in political and academic debates, reality shows, social media exchanges and other, even softer, spaces. It "urges us to respond to the world—and the people in it—in an adversarial frame of mind [and] rests on the assumption that opposition is the best way to get anything done" (ibid.:3–4).

Of course there are exceptions, such as the various models of public and community media, for example (see Dahlgren & Sparks, 1992; Filson, 1992; Habermas, 1962), which strive to overcome the more extreme forms of adversarial debate yet do not necessarily or always transcend inherently conflictual ways of conceptualizing human affairs. Other exceptions are found in the mainstream, where there has been a surge of collaborative reality television programs. These offer a refreshing alternative to their more conflict-driven counterparts but their deeper conceptions of power are also problematic as they reveal adversarial underpinnings. They suggest that power is something to be had and then bestowed—albeit benevolently. In some home renovation programs, for example, a deserving family who has suffered personal tragedy and struggles with its housing situation might receive a high-end home from the broadcaster with some help from the community. In a staggering number of cases, however, the family's financial situation worsens once camera crews leave and it is left with a home for which it has no means or habits of upkeep (see Grondahl, 2011). This betrays material understandings of power, where power resides in the hands of some at the expense of others. Though I provide a more comprehensive discussion of this in the next chapter, I want to mention here that the *ubuntu* concept of power as co-created and mutually empowering force or as "power-sharing" (Louw, 2010) offers a refreshing alternative that distinguishes itself from predominant conceptions in noteworthy ways.

So even efforts to collaborate are often couched within and restricted by the greater reality of normative adversarialism, the roots of which may lie in Kantian and utilitarian ethics. These are characteristically (though not exclusively) individualist and locate "basic moral value in properties intrinsic to a person" (Metz, 2014a:147). In contrast, the ethical thought that is salient amongst sub-Saharan peoples and those in many other countries is chiefly relational (Metz, 2014a:146). Without denying that conflict exists or that conflictual discourses may have merit, such values can provide an alternative realism from which to reshape discourses.

One such value is *ubuntu*. While some will question the link (see for example Richardson, 2008), *ubuntu* is often associated with the more or less non-violent transition of South Africa from *apartheid* to democracy. This process was "the result of the emergence of an ethos of solidarity, a commitment to peaceful co-existence" (Louw, 2010:2). Though the idea of *ubuntu* is more prominent in sub-Saharan belief systems (Metz, 2015), it is not merely African but has a universal dimension and addresses some fundamental principles about human nature, which are helpful to contemporary social thought (see Shutte, 1993:xii). According to Ramose (2002:230–232), "*Ubuntu* is the root of African philosophy", upon which "the fundamental ethical, social, and legal judgment of human worth and human conduct is based". *Ubuntu* is an expression of daily living and a way of knowing that fosters a journey toward "becoming human" (Vanier, 1998).

Of course there are those who maintain that *ubuntu* as a moral philosophy is too vague, "cannot be codified" and is to be understood only on an intuitive "know it when I see it" (Mokgoro, 1998:2) basis. Yet others have attempted to theorize it as a normative moral theory and it is in this context that I see *ubuntu* as a compelling alternative to normative adversarialism. In other words, my focus is not on how *ubuntu* has played out. I am well aware that it has been invoked at times to condone violence in respect to non-conformity (see Mbigi & Maree, 1995). Marx (2002), for example, criticizes how *ubuntu* has been appropriated to sustain a conformist nationalist ideology that glorifies an imagined past. And there are other historic applications that are problematic, such as the exclusion of women from traditional *indabas*, or community gatherings. From today's perspective, these practices contradict *ubuntu*'s egalitarian premise. Yet they are not unique to African societies. Women elsewhere in the West and beyond have also been disenfranchised and it is only since the latter half of the 19th century that collective consciousness has evolved in this regard. As all peoples of the world, "Africans, who are associated with an *ubuntu* philosophy [. . .] are paradigmatic victims" (and perpetrators) "of violent regimes of grotesque acts of war" (Chasi, 2014a:293). Therefore, precisely because we struggle with our lower nature "it is worthwhile that the African moral philosophy of *ubuntu* says people should seek the beautiful, great and good" (Chasi, 2014a:287). As such, I believe that the scholarship on *ubuntu* goes far in discrediting the prevalent assumption that human nature is exclusively and inherently marked by oppression and conflict. It suggests that cultural contexts and discursive formations can also favor collaboration and cooperation. It is simply a matter of choice and nurture. This is reflected in the fact that not all journalism and media and certainly not all aspects of Western liberal society emphasize conflict. Therefore, my interest lies in how *ubuntu* "should [. . .] be understood and utilized" (Louw, 2010:17), which is an ongoing project. "*Ubuntu* is open to interpretation" (Blankenberg, 1999:43) and is "still in the making" (Wiredu, 1980:36).

Ubuntu, which also means 'humanness' in Zulu, Xhosa and other Nguni languages of Southern Africa, implies that the purpose of human existence is "to belong and to participate" (Mkhize, 2008:39–40). "Individuals consider themselves integral parts of the whole community. A person is socialized to think of himself or herself as inextricably bound to others" (Mnyaka & Motlhabi, 2009:69). In this way, *Ubuntu* is descriptive of our social relationships and has a normative dimension that prescribes self-realization through communal, harmonious or cohesive ways of relating (Metz, 2011; Metz & Gaie, 2010; Mnyaka & Motlhabi, 2005). In clarifying this dynamic, Metz (2015:77) stresses the two recurrent themes of 'identity' and 'solidarity', one referring to a closeness of "experiencing life as bound up with others" and the other to a commitment towards others' needs and "acting for others' good". The more one exhibits these characteristics, the more human one becomes. What this implies is that there are two ways of living. One is to give way to one's lower, animal nature and one is to strive toward a higher, genuinely noble way that all humans have the capacity to attain (Bhengu, 1996:27). This (self-) realization of one's higher nature is achieved by exhibiting other-regard, or more specifically, by nurturing communal, harmonious or cohesive relationships with others (Metz & Gaie, 2010:275; Mnyaka & Motlhabi, 2005:222–228). In other words, "The more fully I am involved in community with others the more completely I am able to realize my own deep desires to the full" (Shutte, 1993:9). Individual identities are thus formed through the social realm.

According to Verhoef and Michel (1997:397), this social realm is negotiated in terms of: "What is right is what connects people together; what separates people is wrong". This is understood as a harmonious interaction between diverse individuals (Metz & Gaie, 2010), where individuals are valued, enjoy freedom of expression and are "not limited to what elders find agreeable" (Chasi, 2014b:495). Here, the image of a musical piece comes to mind, where each note can only realize its full potential within the harmonious collaboration (rather than competition) of the various musical notes (Tavernaro-Haidarian, 2018). The individual is treated "as special in virtue of her capacity to enter into relationships of identity and solidarity" (Metz, 2015:78). This relationalism is located between 'individualism' and 'holism' and embodies a concept of unity in diversity where promoting others' welfare includes improving their character or making them better people (see Metz, 2015:79; Shutte, 2001:8–9). As Christians (2004:244) suggests, *ubuntu*'s "commitment to humans as participatory beings avoids the opposition between individualism and collectivism by its unity-in-multiplicity".

A diversely constituted idea of unity also emerges in Metz's (2007, 2014b) quest to define the most justified normative theory of right action with an African pedigree. In this regard he identifies "the requirement to produce harmony and to reduce discord" by fostering a diversely constituted 'we' identity, by coordinating behavior and realizing shared ends (see Metz, 2014b:6763). In *ubuntu*, this overarching sense of 'we' supersedes but also honors other, nested and textured identities within it (see Louw, 2010) and people act in ways that benefit others in mutually reciprocal ways (Metz, 2014b:6763).

This form of identity and solidarity is often associated with the concept of consensus, which features strongly in African philosophy. "In many small-scale African communities, discussion continues until a compromise is found and all in the discussion agree with the outcome" (Metz, 2007:324). Here, Blankenberg (1999:46) refers to the process of *pungwe*, which is a traditional approach to discourse where communities get together to consult on matters and explore solutions. Most notably, the leadership function is shared, "as it becomes a process of learning for both 'facilitator' and 'participant'" (Blankenberg, 1999:46). All members of the community pitch in and decisions are arrived at "by consensus, incorporating both majority and minority viewpoints" (ibid.). Some extend the principles underpinning this form of decision-making to democratic governance, proposing non-partisan models of democracy where candidates do not answer to a constituency but rather to the community as a whole (see Wiredu, 1996:135).

While skeptics of this approach may argue that consensus-oriented decision-making pressures a minority and can lead to collectivism, I submit that this perception derives from within a common sense realism of normative adversarialism, in which power is seen as inherently conflictual and democracy has become synonymous with the concept of partisanship even though there is no necessary correlation between the two (Karlberg, 2004:43). Partisan democracy is a culturally specific model of democracy that has been naturalized in Western societies and is closely linked with the evolution of capitalist economies (ibid.). Both are gleaned from the assumption that people are essentially selfish and competitive and that it is normal and necessary to structure politics as contests. Such a perception also implies that potential abuses of power can be addressed by putting the media in the role of watchdog (Tavernaro-Haidarian, 2018). From within this view and fueled by deficit discourses on Africa, which posit that Africa 'needs to be taught', the only legitimate method for achieving this kind of democracy is that which fuels economic development in terms of Western ideals of modernization and industrialization (see Swanson, 2012). In the *ubuntu* conception of the world, however, which assumes that human interests are not divergent but inherently bound-up and interrelated, partisan power struggles lose their meaning. The goal is to work toward the greater good of others, even if this comes at somewhat of a material price to the individual:

> Actions are not merely those likely to be beneficial, that is to improve the other's state, but also are ones done consequent to certain motives, say for the sake of making the other better off or even a better person.
>
> (Metz, 2015:77)

Within this conception, defeating opponents and winning political campaigns or debates becomes counter-productive. Instead, the aim of mass-mediated public discourse becomes to serve public interest, even "at some cost to profits" (Metz, 2015:82). It is this very sense of community, caring and love for fellow human beings that offers a powerful contribution to reimagining democracy and reveals that the "rationale of decision by consensus [is] to forestall the trivialization of the right of the minority to have an effect on decision-making" (Wiredu, 2002:317).

Through the lens of *ubuntu*, then, discourses do not primarily pan out as arguments. They strive, instead, for consensus and include as many voices as possible in the process. Minorities become valuable rather than marginalized. The mediation of discourse happens in a "facilitatory manner and must be consultative and ongoing" (Blankenberg, 1999:45). *Ubuntu* cultivates respect for particularity and entails being with others (Louw, 2010:15). Diversity is valued and not seen as a source of conflict. Rather, participants of a discourse agree to disagree when consensus cannot be found (Louw, 2001), as the preservation of relations or unity is deemed more valuable than adherence to personal views or economic and material wellbeing (Metz, 2009). Ultimately, *ubuntu* cultivates cohesion and mutual exposure. Its central premise is participation as an element of connection, which unites in its diversity elements "of the visible and invisible worlds" (Bhengu, 1996:38).

This is also reflected in the scholarship that considers *ubuntu* and journalism ethics. Here, the role of journalists, media producers, media houses, the government and other stakeholders is seen to enable and foster "communal relationships between residents themselves as well as between residents and the state" and any other groups or individuals such as businesses and civil society organizations (Metz, 2015:83). As Wasserman (2013:78) suggests:

> Treating all people with human dignity means they should not be viewed as a means to the ends of adversarial, watchdog-type journalism, but as ends in themselves. This entails listening to their stories— their narratives about their every day lives.

Broadly then, the idea of an *ubuntu* journalism is located within a public service *ethos* (Rodny-Gumede, 2015) and moves from the realm of libertarian objectivity, where journalists become brokers, to the realm of 'authentic disclosure' (Christians, 2004), where journalists become mediators that take into account multiple interpretations and cultural complexities (Duncan &

Seloane, 1998). In this sense, audiences broaden and a wider set of interests and concerns are opened up (Rodny-Gumede, 2015). Citizens are empowered to become active participants in the process of self-governance (Christians, 2004). This "empowers citizens to come to agreement about social problems and solutions among themselves rather than depending on the political elite or professional experts" (Christians, 2004:235) and is achieved by focusing on a wide range of viewpoints.

In order to cultivate this, Wasserman (2013) proposes that communicators momentarily remove themselves from the discussion so that they can really listen to the perspectives of others. In defining and describing this vital approach, however, which takes into consideration a diverse array of what he calls "divergent" interests and voices, Wasserman (2013) says he seeks to make democratic media an "area of contestation and struggle" in order to "break the elite continuity" in post-*apartheid* South Africa. This particular description of a vital project, then, could be seen as engendering more of a normative adversarial attitude rather than an *ubuntu*-based one. Notions of 'struggle' and 'contestation', 'secession', 'dismantling', 'reacting' and 'rejecting' are informed by adversarial codes. Rather, in an *ubuntu*-inspired realism, a deliberative and exploratory form of journalism could 'celebrate' diverse views as 'bound-up' instead of 'divergent' and work toward 'integrating' these into an all-inclusive discourse. Such may be a far more effective response to elite continuity.

In light of the above, the aforementioned 'dismantling' or 'social protest' frame for decolonization can in fact be seen as deepening coloniality by employing the very strategies it seeks to replace. Instead, framing decolonization as a developmental process of 'maturation' or 'evolution' becomes a more powerful approach for transcending coloniality and the strategies we have inherited through it.

In this vein, Wasserman's description of an 'ethics of listening', where the media become gate-openers rather than gate-keepers, and his call to "look for ways in which our narratives are connected, interrelated and interdependent" (Wasserman, 2013:78–79) are particularly well articulated to foreground the deeply relational aspects of *ubuntu*. Of course listening or deliberating within a normative framework of *ubuntu* need not be a cozy and artificially polite undertaking but rather one of frank and critical yet fundamentally mutualistic engagement. The rhetorical approach implied here is a consultative, exploratory one that enables a wide array of complementary views rather than the chiefly persuasive and reductionist approach of mainstream discourses.

Because of this, *ubuntu* scholars argue for a move away from Western notions of objectivity toward the idea of a "multifarious subjectivity", where many views are represented and "grounded historically and bio-graphically" so that "interpretative accounts reflect genuine features of the situation under investigation, and not [. . .] the aberrations or hurried conclusions of observer opinions" (Christians, 2004:247). In this form of journalism, the citizen is put in the active role of "participant in the process of self-governance" (Carey, 1997:139). According to Fourie (2011:38), the journalist "is not an observer" but rather an "active member" and a partici-pant of the community and its discourses. "Beyond facilitating a sense of togetherness and joint progress" (Metz, 2015:83) for citizens, the media and mediators should also "aim to serve the transformation of society" (Wasser-man & De Beer, 2005:202).

In summary then, the descriptive/prescriptive approach of *ubuntu* opens up "a space for the concerns, ideas and opinions of the community [. . .] stim-ulating citizen participation, community participation and consensus based on widespread consultation with the community" (Fourie, 2011:37). With all this in mind, the normative moral theory of *ubuntu* can play a significant role in reshaping and transforming contemporary discourses. It provides an organic worldview of harmony and coordination and operates on the assump-tion that human nature is profoundly relational and other-oriented rather than selfish. "*Ubuntu* ethics can be termed anti-egoistic as it discourages people from seeking their own good without regard for, or to the detriment of, oth-ers and the community" (Mnyaka & Motlhabi, 2009:71–72). A normative mutualism of this nature could significantly transform the processes and structures, messages and models of contemporary public discourse.

Of course one need only look at parliamentary debates in South Africa, the United States and elsewhere in the world, to see that we do not live in a society where *ubuntu* or any other harmonious value-system serves as an overarching realism. While elements of oneness and interconnectivity are doubtlessly present and emerge in various contexts, such as the South African constitution or the American national anthem, they don't form a deeply internalized reality or framework (Tavernaro-Haidarian, 2018). In her 2015 survey, Rodny-Gumede (2015:123) confirms that most journalists in South Africa have a vague understanding of how *ubuntu* would practically translate into their work and there is a fear of it being used as a Trojan horse to push the political agenda of the government. In that regard, they still view themselves as watchdogs of (adversarial notions of) power, while striving to achieve a higher degree of community involvement. A real gap remains in the translation of *ubuntu* principles into practice.

This is where efforts to articulate alternative models of public discourse become vital. When considering communication that is based in relational, harmonious and cohesive understandings of power that "cannot be achieved apart from others" (Metz, 2014b:6762), it is possible to create very different talk show models and reality television formats, to explore new ways of hosting political discussions and to innovate methodologically throughout the realm of communication and media, transforming both how we perceive reality and how we continue to create it. In order to do so, my next chapters take a closer look at how power becomes operative in contemporary discourses and what some of the formal properties of discourse might look like through the lens of *ubuntu*.

References

Bhengu, M.J. (1996). *Ubuntu: The Essence of Democracy*. Cape Town: Novalis.

Blankenberg, N. (1999). In Search of Real Freedom: Ubuntu and the Media. *Critical Arts*, 12(2):42–65.

Booysen, S. (ed) (2016). *Fees Must Fall*. Johannesburg: Wits University Press.

Carey, J.W. (1997). The Communication Revolution and the Professional Communicator: Afterword: The Culture in Question. In Munson, E.S. & Warren, C.A. (eds). *James Carey: A Critical Reader*: 128–143, 308–339, Minneapolis: University of Minnesota Press.

Chasi, C. (2014a). Violent Communication Is Not Alien to Ubuntu: Nothing Human Is Alien to Africans. *Communicatio: South African Journal for Communication Theory and Research*, 40(4):287–304.

Chasi, C. (2014b). Ubuntu and Freedom of Expression. *Ethics & Behavior*, 24(6): 495–509.

Christians, C.G. (2004). Ubuntu and Communitarianism in Media Ethics. *Ecquid Novi*, 25(2):235–256.

Dahlgren, P. & Sparks, C. (1992). *Journalism and Popular Culture*. London: Sage.

Derrida, J. (1978). *Writing and Difference*. Chicago: University of Chicago Press.

Duncan, J. & Seloane, M. (1998). Introduction. In Duncan, J. & Seloane, M. (eds). *Media and Democracy in South Africa*: 1–53, Pretoria: HSRC.

Fairclough, N.L. & Wodak, R. (1997). Critical Discourse Analysis. In Van Dijk, T.A. (ed). *Discourse Studies: A Multidisciplinary Introduction (2): Discourse as Social Interaction*. London: Sage.

Filson, G. (1992). Cooperative Inquiry as a Theory of Practice: Contributions of John Dewey and Jurgen Habermas, Doctoral Dissertation, Toronto, Canada: University of Toronto.

Foucault, M. (1972). *The Archeology of Knowledge*. London: Tavistock.

Foucault, M. (1980). *Power/Knowledge*. Brighton: Harvester.

Fourie, P. (2011). Normative Media Theory in a Changed Media Landscape and Globalized Society. In Hyde-Clarke, N. (ed). *Communication and Media Ethics in South Africa*: 25–45, Cape Town: Juta.

Grondahl, P. (2011). No Fairy Tale Ending for 'Extreme Makeover' Family. *Times Union*, 9 March 2011, www.timesunion.com/local/article/No-fairy-tale-ending-for-Exteme-Makeover-family-1044410.php, Accessed 15 May 2017.

Habermas, J. (1989/1962). *The Structural Transformation of the Public Sphere*. Boston: MIT.

Isaacs De Vega, T.J. (2017). The Meaning of Decolonization for Media Studies: Rethinking Journalism Theory and Education in Post-Apartheid South Africa, Pan Discussion, South African Communication Association Conference, 21 August–1 September 2017, Grahamstown, South Africa.

Karlberg, M. (1997). News and Conflict: How Adversarial News Frames Limit Public Understanding of Environmental Issues. *Alternatives Journal*, 23(1):22–27.

Karlberg, M. (2004). *Beyond the Culture of Contest*. Oxford: George Ronald.

Karlberg, M. (2005). The Power of Discourse and the Discourse of Power: Pursuing Peace through Discourse Intervention. *International Journal of Peace Studies*, 10(1):1–25.

Louw, D.J. (2001). Ubuntu and the Challenge of Multiculturalism in Post-Apartheid South Africa, Unitwin Student Network, 2001, www.phys.uu.nl/˜unitwin/, Accessed 4 November 2014.

Louw, D.J. (2010). Power Sharing and the Challenge of Ubuntu Ethics, Paper presented at the Forum for Religious Dialogue Symposium of the Research Institute for Theology and Religion at the University of South Africa, January 2010, Pretoria, South Africa.

Marx, C. (2002). Ubu and Ubuntu: On the Dialectics of Apartheid and Nation Building. *Politikon: South African Journal of Political Studies*, 29(1):49–69.

Mbigi, L. & Maree, J. (1995). *Ubuntu: The Spirit of African Transformation Management*. Randburg: Knowledge Resources.

Metz. T. (2007). Toward an African Moral Theory. *Journal of Political Philosophy*, 15(1):321–341.

Metz, T. (2009). African Moral Theory and Public Governance: Nepotism, Preferential Hiring and Other Partiality. In Munyaradzi, F.M. (ed). *African Ethics: An Anthology for Comparative and Applied Ethics*: 335–356, Pietermaritzburg: University of KwaZulu-Natal Press.

Metz, T. (2011). Ubuntu as a Moral Theory and Human Rights in South Africa. *African Human Rights Law Journal*, 11(1):532–559.

Metz, T. (2014a). Harmonizing Global Ethics in the Future: A Proposal to Add South and East to West. *Journal of Global Ethics*, 10(2):146–155.

Metz, T. (2014b). Ubuntu: The Good Life. In Michalos, A. (ed). *Encyclopedia of Quality of Life and Well-Being Research*. Dordrecht: Springer.

Metz, T. (2015). African Ethics and Journalism Ethics: News and Opinion in Light of Ubuntu. *Journal of Media Ethics: Exploring Questions of Media Morality*, 30(2):74–90.

Metz, T. (2016). The South African Student/Worker Protests in the Light of Just War Theory. In Booysen, S. (ed). *Fees Must Fall*: 293–306, Johannesburg: Wits University Press.

Metz, T. & Gaie, J. (2010). The African Ethic of Ubuntu/Botho: Implications for Research on Morality. *Journal of Moral Education*, 39(1):273–290.

Mkhize, N. (2008). Ubuntu and Harmony: An African Approach to Morality and Ethics. In Nicolson, R. (ed). *Persons in Community: African Ethics in a Global Culture*: 35–44, Pietermaritzburg: University of KwaZulu-Natal Press.

Mnyaka, M. & Motlhabi, M. (2005). The African Concept of Ubuntu/Botho and Its Socio-Moral Significance. *Black Theology*, 3(1):215–237.

Mnyaka, M. & Motlhabi, M. (2009). Ubuntu and Its Socio-Moral Significance. In Murove, M.F. (ed). *African Ethics: An Anthology of Comparative and Applied Ethics*: 63–84, Pietermaritzburg: University of KwaZulu-Natal Press.

Mokgoro, Y. (1998). Ubuntu and the Law in South Africa. *Potchefstroom Electronic Law Journal*, 1(1):1–11.

Phillips, N. & Hardy, C. (2002). *Discourse Analysis: Investigating Process of Social Construction*. Thousand Oaks: Sage.

Ramose, M.B. (2002). *African Philosophy Through Ubuntu*. Harare: Mond Books.

Rao, S. & Wasserman, H. (2007). Global Media Ethics Revisited: A Postcolonial Critique. *Global Media and Communication*, 3(1):29–50.

Richardson, R.N. (2008). Reflections on Reconciliation and Ubuntu. In Nicolson, R. (ed). *Persons in Community: African Ethics in a Global Culture*: 65–83, Scottsville: University of KwaZulu-Natal Press.

Rodny-Gumede, Y. (2015). An Assessment of the Public Interest and Ideas of the Public in South Africa and the Adoption of Ubuntu Journalism. *Journal of Mass Media Ethics*, 30(2):109–124.

Shutte, A. (1993). *Philosophy for Africa*. Cape Town: University of Cape Town Press.

Shutte, A. (2001). *Ubuntu: An Ethic for the New South Africa*. Cape Town: Cluster Publications.

Swanson, D.M. (2012). Ubuntu, African Epistemology and Development: Contributions, Tensions, Contradictions and Possibilities. In Wright, H.K. & Abdi, A.A. (eds). *The Dialectics of African Education and Western Discourses: Appropriation, Ambivalence and Alternatives*: 27–52, New York: Peter Lang.

Tannen, D. (1998). *The Argument Culture*. New York: Random House.

Tavernaro-Haidarian, L. (2018). Ubuntu and the Communication Power Nexus. In Mutsvairo, B. (ed). *Palgrave Handbook for Media and Communication Research in Africa*. London: Palgrave Macmillan.

Tomaselli, K.G. (2003). Our Culture vs Foreign Culture. *Gazette: International Journal for Communication Studies*, 65(6):427–444.

Vanier, J. (1998). *Becoming Human*. Toronto: Anasi.

Verhoef, H. & Michel, C. (1997). Studying Morality within the African Context: A Model of Moral Analysis and Construction. *Journal of Moral Education*, 26(4):389–407.

Wasserman, H. (2013). Journalism in a New Democracy: The Ethics of Listening. *Communicatio: South African Journal for Communication Theory and Research*, 39(1):67–84.

Wasserman, H. & De Beer, A.S. (2005). Which Public? Whose Interest? The South African Media and Its Role during the First Ten Years of Democracy. *Critical Arts*, 19(1–2):36–51.

Wiredu, K. (1980). *Philosophy and an African Culture*. Cambridge: Cambridge University Press.

Wiredu, K. (1996). *Cultural Universals and Particulars: An African Perspective*. Bloomington: Indiana University Press.

Wiredu, K. (2002). The Moral Foundations of an African Culture. In Coetzee, P.H. & Roux, P.J. (eds). *The African Philosophy Reader*. London: Routledge.

2   Discourse, Power and *Ubuntu*

The adversarial paradigm that permeates much of our thinking and doing in the global North is closely related to a specific conception of power. Power is mostly (though not always consciously) thought of in conflictual terms and associated with material resources. It is seen as something that can rest in the hands of a group or a person in equal or unequal measure and is relegated to the level of worldly affairs. However, this conception of power is not always the most relevant. While revealing a significant facet of the complexity at hand there are other, reciprocal and relational ways of conceiving power that unfold as energy, agency or on the level of spiritual reality. Considering how contemporary societies are interconnected through global trade and industry, through virtual and transnational currencies and most importantly through an all-encompassing network of communication that knows no boundaries, such dimensions of power are no less real. They help us reconsider the way we relate as human beings and how we could organize to address the more material inequalities that exist. In this chapter, I mention some alternative ways for thinking of power that emerge both from the global North and the global South and focus particularly on the locution implied by *ubuntu*, which can significantly reshape processes of communication toward relational ends.

A condensed way of summarizing how power has predominantly been discussed in Western literature is to distinguish between the ideas of 'power to' and 'power over' (Connolly, 1974; Dowding, 1996; Karlberg, 2005; Lukes, 1986; Macpherson, 1973; Tavernaro-Haidarian, 2018). These concepts point to "two fundamentally different ordinary-language locutions within which the term 'power' occurs" (Wartenberg, 1990:27). One expresses the idea of capacity (see for example Lukes, 1986; Wartenberg, 1990) and the other focuses on how this capacity may be channeled toward exercising dominion over others, for example through "territory, military capacity and economic wealth" (Ramsbotham, 2010:170).

While some attention has been given to the idea of power as force or capacity rather than substance or matter (see for example Wrong, 1968; Foucault, 1980), the social and political sciences tend to highlight the latter locution and all the ways in which it can manifest, arguing that ideas of force and capacity generally deflect from the pressing material inequalities that exist in the socio-political realm and hence from that which discourses of power should ultimately focus on (see Foucault, 1980; Lukes, 1986; Wartenberg, 1990; Wrong, 1968). Such inequalities also "shape the agenda for African nations on 'survival', 'recovery' and 'catching up' to the competitive advantage of more powerful nations" (Swanson, 2012:32). Scholars write also of 'threat', 'bargaining', 'intercursive' or 'integrative' power (Boulding, 1990; Wrong, 1968:674). Interestingly, 'integrative' does not imply a reciprocal coming together relationship but rather one where a party may surrender to the other. Such adversarial manifestations of power can end in stalemates if they are equally strong and directed against each other. They are characterized by conflict, control and coercion (see for example Bourdieu, 1994; Machiavelli, 1961; Weber, 1986) and are related to Hobbesian and Marxist conceptions:

> Darwin, Nietzsche, Marx and Freud all based their thinking on conflict theories. For Machiavelli, conflict is a result of the human desire for self-preservation and power [. . .]; for Hobbes, the three 'principle causes of quarrel' in a state of nature are competition for gain, fear of insecurity, and the defense of honor; for Hume the underlying conditions for human conflict are relative resource scarcity and limited altruism; for Rousseau, the 'state of war' is born from the 'social state' itself and so on.
>
> (Ramsbotham, 2010:33)

However, depending, as Wartenberg (1990:27) proposes, "upon which locution one takes as the basis of one's theory of power, one will arrive at a very different model of the role of power in the social world". In light of the pressing material inequalities that theorists aptly describe and legitimately want to tackle, it is important to look at the literature that provides some nuance as a way of generating new solutions. Giddens (1984:257), for example, suggests that "power is not necessarily linked with conflict [. . .] and is not inherently oppressive". Similar ideas can be derived from the capability approach, which emphasizes one's empowerment in terms of the capability to live a life one may value and which depends on the conditions for potential rather than actual actions (see Nussbaum, 2011). According to Metz (2014:148) Nussbaum's capability approach unearths explicitly relational facets, as "a person must be assured of the ability to relate positively to other human beings and animals". And while it is not feasible to summarize the texture and range that exists within the various traditions of feminism, it can be said that ideas such as capability, force and energy also emerge from within its literature alongside ideas of resistance from domination.

For example, some feminist scholars discuss how power is created (see Collins, 1990; Crenshaw, 2015; Lorde, 1984) and others describe the relationship between energy and community (see Collins, 1990). Some theorize on the collaborative aspects of power (see also Arendt, 1969; Hartsock, 1983; Miller, 1982) and others discuss how this complements the more competitive and aggressive conceptions of power that favor male privilege (see Brocke-Utne, 1989; Moulton, 1983). Black feminist thought in particular has also included class and race within the broader categories of 'women' and 'power' (see Amos & Parmar, 1984; Collins, 1990; Crenshaw, 2015; Parmar, 1990). It thematizes the simultaneity class, race and gender and integrates these aspects in such a way that illuminates how "all groups possess varying amounts of penalty and privilege in one historically created system" (Collins, 1990:223). From this vantage point, White women can be seen as disadvantaged through gender but privileged through race, as "domination operates not only from the top down but also by annexing the power as energy of those on the bottom for its own ends" (Crenshaw, 2015:21).

What all of these impulses suggest is that power can be thought of as a complex reality with a breadth of facets that can be operationalized in a number of different ways, depending on where one stands. They can manifest in material terms or as energy and often times as both. And if authoritative and oppressive locutions of power form one extreme end of this gamut, then the other may be characterized by deeply cohesive and relational ones as found in *ubuntu* (Tavernaro-Haidarian, 2018). These can be conceptualized as "circular, organic, and collectivist, rather than linear, unitized, materialistic, and individualistic" (Swanson, 2012:37).

One of the reasons *ubuntu* lends itself as a focus of study for such harmonious notions is its implied relationship with South Africa's peaceful transition to democracy. This is arguably one of the most noteworthy political accomplishments of recent history. And in order to shed light on the implications of this event for conceptualizing power, I consider how South

Africa managed to peacefully negotiate for "a poor majority to [. . .] share power with a rich minority" (Sommer, 1996:53).

According to Moriarty (2003:3) this occurred "because its political leaders changed the way they talked about the political scene". Of course, such a process would have unfolded in both directions as changes in political rhetoric influenced actions and actions influenced rhetoric. Moriarty, however, focuses on how South African political reality was transformed by the changes that occurred in the way political leaders spoke of that reality, how they rhetorically addressed major political players and how they defined the relationships between them. He proposes that the more conflictual and violent this relationship was characterized as, the more violent their actions toward each other became and vice versa. In turn, the more each side was rhetorically humanized by the other, the more peaceful their relationship became. In other words, as discourse became increasingly relational so did political reality. Again, I would assume that the political language of the time was, in turn, also affected by the actions of key players in a feedback process that is characteristic of human discourse and social practice and that can be evidenced throughout human history, unfolding along a collaborative trajectory: Societies have always been characterized by an increasing degree of cooperation and relationalism, which has allowed us to go from small-scale to large-scale communities; from tribal formations to city-states and from nations to international unions. And as such, alternative conceptions of power have also played a significant role—not necessarily as expressions of voluntary cohesion but sometimes as evolutionary necessity.

In this vein, Read (2010:335) suggests that in the case of 1990s South Africa not all were in fact motivated by the vision of a racially inclusive country. Instead, it was their fear of civil war or of complete obliteration that forced them to consider negotiations for what seemed like a lesser evil in the form of a free South Africa for all—Whites included. So it was not in all cases good will or the desire to cooperate but ultimately the idea that both sides had more to gain from cooperating than maintaining their divisive stance, which eventually resulted in a peaceful transition. He refers to this conflict as being defined by variable-sum rather than zero-sum dynamics, raising questions about the very nature of power:

> One of the fundamental and still-contested questions in the literature on power is whether power should be seen in zero-sum, purely relative terms—one side's gain entailing by definition another's loss, because power means dominating someone else ('power-over'), or whether

power should be understood as variable-sum: collectively gained and collectively lost, because power means the capacity to accomplish some goal ('power-to') which may be shared.

(Read, 2010:319)

Here, Read (2010) extends the idea of capacity to include shared ends, uncovering some of the many subtleties that can and must be acknowledged when thinking of power. Of course both zero-sum and variable-sum relations describe vital aspects of how power can be theorized and both can be important in understanding its contextual and operational facets more fully. This is also true for many other meanings that power can have. For example, religious or spiritual connotations exist that involve the 'power to' exert 'power over' the self. Specifically, notions such as self-discipline, sacrifice or even surrender and acceptance are understood in some contexts as the ultimate expressions of power because they champion the 'lower self' or the ego and empower the 'higher self' or the spirit (see Tolle, 2005). Relationships between loved ones are often characterized in this way. In a political or economic context, however, such ideas may be conceptualized as sheer disempowerment, although it can also be argued that leaders such as Mahatma Gandhi and Nelson Mandela employed elements of 'power over self' in order to further non-violent political goals. What all these examples show, then, is that the lines are clearly blurred when it comes to the reality of power and only in theory and to refashion socio-political realities can we dissect its facets.

In this light, though Read (2010) points out that conflict was also very much present during South Africa's political transition, it is possible to conceive of this moment as a greater case of cooperation. Various sides or factions ultimately came to the realization that it was in their own common interest to collaborate. The situation was thus framed as a shared problem and key stakeholders adopted the view that existing strategies would lead to an impasse. This suggests that the more variable-sum aspects of power deserve attention for achieving maximum outcomes for diverse populations where chiefly zero-sum notions have reached a point of diminishing returns.

Of course, depending on whether one is motivated by a sincere desire to collaborate or chooses this as a lesser evil, the sustainability of the situation will vary. Where individuals and groups are primarily motivated by sectarian interests and short-term gratification, making sustained sacrifices for the long-term good of a larger community does not make sense, unity becomes volatile and conditional and a primarily individualist *ethos* kicks in.

By contrast, and while "Western individualist democracy insists on freedom [. . .] of the sacred self from intrusion by others", in *ubuntu*, "a person's freedom depends for its exercise and fulfilment on personal relationships with others" (Christians, 2004:243). This profoundly bound-up conception of power is operationalized as the freedom to articulate and optimally pursue what the community envisions collectively (Blankenberg, 1999:47). In this way, South Africa's transition to democracy can also be seen as a case where the commitment to unity outweighed the idea of shared ends as a lesser evil and where this was "not merely the result of the compromises reached by politicians through negotiations" (Louw, 2010:2). Negotiations, which imply the patching up of conflicting interests into a tolerable action plan, evolved into a process where a range of interests were harmoniously integrated into a more congruent polity.

In light of contemporary developments, however, it remains to be seen if this commitment to peaceful harmony and cohesion is strong enough to withstand the waves of disunity, corruption and greed that currently assail South Africa. The detachment of many in the new South African elite from issues of poverty and access facing their fellow citizens undermines any attempt at significant social and socio-economic reconstruction. This is where reclaiming talk associated with *ubuntu* continues to play a vital role.

The conception of power implied by *ubuntu* derives from immaterial energy rather than from material resources such as wealth, weapons, physical strength or natural resources. As Tempels explains, wherever European philosophy would think primarily of substance, traditional African thought thinks first of force (Tempels in Shutte, 1993:52) or "vital force in participation" (Setiloane, 1993:55). In interpreting Tempels's account of vital force, Chasi (2014:290) proposes that, "Africans traditionally understand that agency or power should be measured in terms of the sustainability of the effects associated with human actions". Sustainability points to that which transcends temporary personal gains or short-term planning horizons and looks instead toward the wellbeing of community and society as a whole. In the *ubuntu* conception of human relations, then, there are no entities but rather fields of forces and "Values, moral commitments, existential meanings are all negotiated dialogically" (Christians, 2004:237).

The idea of 'we' implied in this conception has vast implications for social practice, favoring, for example, collective decision-making processes and non-partisan governance. It is also reflected in Metz's (2015:77) view that *ubuntu* finds expression in an overarching ('we') identity and in solidarity toward this identity, which entails mutually beneficial actions. Power and agency are thus generated through concerted action. Within this integral network of relationships freedom is not the right of individuals alone, rather "freedom of expression means a community is able to freely articulate its questions and concerns" (Blankenberg, 1999:47). A community is therefore characterized by mutuality and reciprocity. As Louw (2001:1) suggests:

> [. . .] it would strictly speaking be misleading to speak of ubuntu *and* power sharing, and more correct to speak of ubuntu *as* power sharing. Ubuntu is power sharing; it constitutes the sharing of power. On this score, the aphorism 'a person is a person through other persons' translates as 'a person is a person through sharing his/her power'—i.e. the space that allows the enactment of his/her subjectivity with other persons.

Because of this very significant way in which it distinguishes itself from traditional ideas around power and because of its African pedigree, *ubuntu* is often associated with a form of resistance or a struggle for power and freedom from colonialism (see Louw, 2010; Tavernaro-Haidarian, 2018). The invocation of an ethic of 'interdependence' and 'unity' for the purpose of 'independence' and 'secession', however, is quite ironic (see ibid.; Van Hensbroek, 1999:201) and can only really be considered in this way through the lens of normative adversarialism. If one were to consider an alternative lens, one of normative mutualism or an *ubuntu* realism as it were, the idea of a 'struggle for power' could be reframed in terms of a 'culmination' or 'fulfillment' of mutual energy (see Tavernaro-Haidarian, 2018).

In this way, the aforementioned idea of decolonization can itself be thought of as a process of collective maturation and as evolutionary rather than revolutionary. In fact decolonization depends, by definition, on the very notion of colonialism and cannot return to something pre-existent, ancient and 'other'. Thus, *ubuntu* as a normative moral theory would pre-scribe working 'with' the status quo rather than against it and would tran-scend coloniality in deeply integrative rather than reactionary ways.

Of course, and this is what Read (2010) refers to when he says that many South Africans were hedging their bets rather than being genuinely invested in the vision of a racially inclusive society; *ubuntu* and related notions of cohesion and harmony do not currently constitute the common sense locution from which we see the world. There are contexts for which they become relevant and there are moments in which we operate from within this realism, but for the most part it still co-exists alongside adversarial frames of mind in fragmented and relative ways (see Tavernaro-Haidarian,

2018). Yet this does not diminish the significance of including harmonious, cohesive and relational notions of power into our overarching understanding of it and it certainly does not diminish the value of any and all efforts to make us conscious of these and to cultivate related social practices. For this reason, it is critical to consider a more expansive way for conceptualizing the broader facets of power—one that reconciles all of its dimensions and is useful as a basis for normative and critical social theory.

In order to do this, and in engaging with and extending what others have begun (see Karlberg, 2005), I consider power as a general umbrella term and subsequently delineate both material and immaterial (or energy based) aspects of power. On the material end of the gamut, the imbalanced idea of domination/submission can be seen as one specific manifestation and the balance of power can be seen as another. Furthermore and regardless of whether it is balanced or imbalanced, this type of material power can be directed for the benefit of someone, as is the case in a helpful or benevolent act, or against someone or something, as is the case in exploitative acts. When it is directed for the benefit of someone it is not necessarily empowering.

An obvious example is giving to a beggar or having a broadcaster build a home for a struggling family. In both cases, material resources are poured into a situation that does not, on its own, facilitate any sustainable empowerment for its beneficiaries. Another possibility is to locate aspects of a parent-child relationship here. A parent has more material power than a child and may nurture it by providing resources such as food, shelter and access to knowledge. In the same way a teacher may instruct her students and provide them with intellectual resources. In both cases, however, this material power can also be used in abusive ways, as was the case in the so-called *bantu* education policies of the 1950s, which essentially legalized the economic slavery of Black people under *apartheid* in South Africa. It enforced racially segregated educational facilities that were devised in a way that would direct Black and Non-White youth to the unskilled labor market, thereby rendering them dependent on the White minority (Byrnes, 1996).

On the other hand, to the extent that teachers or mothers (also) empower their students in immaterial ways, say in psycho-social, spiritual or values-based ways, other notions of power come into play.

Here the immaterial, energy-based and relational aspects of power emerge that we might find on the other end of the spectrum. In the *ubuntu* conception of human relations, power is a "universal field" where "humanity occupies the central place" and "both spirit and matter (are) aspects of a more fundamental energy that is continually producing and developing persons throughout their lives, from birth to death" (Shutte, 2001:8, 12). In *ubuntu*, power "is understood as the empowerment of mutuality" (Christians, 2004:245) and is thus channeled toward the greater good of all. This resolves the I/other dichotomy of power where, through *ubuntu*, power is seen as that which grows between people and expands the more it includes rather than excludes. As Setiloane explains, "The essence of being is participation in which humans are always interlocked with one another. The human being is not only 'vital force' but 'vital force in participation'" (Setiloane, 1993:55). Being an individual in this context "means being with others" and being with others is not added onto "a pre-existent and self-sufficient being; rather, both this being (the self) and the others find themselves in a whole wherein they are already related" (Macquarrie, 1972:104). The world is conceived of as a matrix or "web of reciprocal relations, in which subject and object become indistinguishable" (Louw, 2001:24), and in which "I think therefore I am" becomes "I participate, therefore I am" (Shutte, 1993:47).

In order to discuss a possible manifestation of this immaterial and relational aspect of power, we can consider an alternative version of the aforementioned home improvement program from Chapter 1. Instead of a group of outsiders coming in with vast amounts of money to make over a house for someone, residents and community members within a shared community can come together to devise, plan and execute a creative and modest make-over on one or several of their own homes. The aim here would be to self-initiate the project and to then cooperate to make the house and neighborhood safer and brighter and to optimize space and utility for its inhabitants using local resources, artisans and recycled materials. Such a project would support and channel joint efforts that are affordable, creative and can be replicated without depending on handouts (see Tavernaro-Haidarian, 2016). Another example can be gleaned by considering discourses that construct 'disadvantage' in school settings. In this regard, Swanson (2012) shares her pedagogic journey as a White South African who is directly implicated in the construal of this frame. In documenting how she looked for less objectifying ways of being in research, Swanson produces a self-reflexive narrative that seeks to understand, deconstruct and decolonize hegemonic meanings in relation to 'disadvantage' in the context of educational development in a township school and to allow for other possibilities of being in the world. She relays recognizing her own (White) "voice of violence, of what brutality I had done in feeding into the deficit discourse, on 'disadvantage'" and that her own thoughts, "framed within the discursive roots of my socialization, had established that 'disadvantage' as 'plain to see'" (ibid.:46). Furthermore:

> I had been taking on the colonizing voice that produces the deficit, and that creates, validates and establishes 'the problem' from outside, from a place out there that can speak unmonitored by its own surveillance'. [. . .] The source of the problem lay silently behind the construction of the 'problem' itself. [. . .] I was complicit with a system that establishes 'truth' on 'deficit' and lays blame.
>
> (Swanson, 2012:46)

In reframing these meanings and the 'deficit discourse' in terms of a collective 'we' from which there is only relationalism rather than 'advantage' and 'disadvantage', Swanson suggests that the 'source' of these meanings is reconsidered and a collective way of 're-sourcing' toward prosperity and healing privileged. Such is a glimpse of the fundamental shift that can occur when we consider the relational notions of power associated with *ubuntu*. The lines of action that are opened in this way are empowering, mutualistic and liberating.

Relational power, then, is something that 'we' create and that 'we' can use to evolve the status quo or to collectively regress. It is not directed at or against an 'other'. Rather, it is generated by and empowering for the collective 'we'. The assumption here is that, even if I have access to more material resources (money, industrial development, infrastructure, weapons of mass destruction), 'we' are still bound by an invisible matrix where your downfall will sooner or later lead to my downfall and vice versa. It is an understanding of agency and power based in its long-term sustainability. This accounts for the exigencies and highly interrelated nature of our modern societies, where a crisis in one area will quickly lead to a crisis in another area. What is bad for the individual will, in the long run (albeit longer for some than others), be bad for society as a whole, which is perhaps one of the reasons for the reconciliatory approach to justice associated with *ubuntu*.

Of course, all of the above-mentioned facets of power are highly and organically interrelated, often operating on multiple levels and at the same time. In other words, the reality of power is as expansive as the reality or science of a leaf. Yet dissecting it into its physical, biological or chemical properties helps us better understand the leaf and address its needs. As such it is possible to discover that a benevolent act of charity is not inherently bad. But rather, that benevolence is valuable in conjunction with other, immaterial, aspects of power and empowerment—certainly an insight many non-governmental/non-profit and charitable organizations share. The knowledge of this multiplicity helps us make a number of distinctions that are often lost in predominant discourses on power and helps us realize the relativity and fluidity of it. By it we can recognize the capacity for relational social practices to enable joint progress and wellbeing. We may even find that those relational aspects are more innate than our conflictual ones and that we can create models of communication that bring out cohesive, harmonious and congruent lines of action rather than eliciting mere compromise. As Christians (2004:246) suggests, "Given the primacy of our relational reality, unless humans use their freedom to help others flourish, they deny their own well-being".

When we reconceive power in this way we can redesign our social strategies. Based on such extended conceptions of power, it is possible to reimagine reality in terms of a complementarity of socio-political issues and interests. *Ubuntu* suggests that thinking and knowing about the world does not have to derive from (largely false) exclusionary or binary frames and in mutually exclusive ways. Our affairs and realities can be thought of as bound-up, complementary and open-ended, encouraging a vast diversity of views and voices. Commonalities and overlaps can be found and emphasized and related social action enabled. From within this worldview, Africa need not be seen as 'lacking' or as 'catching up' to the unbridled drive for creating individual prosperity and self-aggrandizement at the expense of others and the environment. Instead, collective interests and prosperity become foregrounded. In terms of the way we exercise power, a broader and more representative wealth of perspectives can enter the public sphere that is not restricted by moneyed interests and dominant parties. This strengthens civic responsibility because it enables citizens to participate fully in public discourse rather than being relegated to the role of spectator or consumer of one brand of thinking or another (Karlberg, 2002). This can increase social cohesion and encourage diverse members of society to enter the political process:

Political processes, like other processes of life, should not remain unaffected by the powers of the human spirit [. . .]: the power of unity, of love, of humble service, of pure deeds. Associated with power in this sense are words such as 'release', 'encourage', 'channel', 'guide' and 'enable'. Power is not a finite entity, which is to be 'seized' and 'jealously guarded'; it constitutes a limitless capacity to transform that, which resides in the human race.

(Bahá'í International Community, 2013:n.p.)

By considering immaterial and relational facets of power, practical models of communication and non-partisan models of governance can emerge that strive for participatory and collective decision-making, where leadership roles are shared and the community is involved in multiple tiers. Media people and journalists need not focus so much on curbing the potential abuses of material power but rather on channeling mutual empowerment and on enabling broader discussions and views that transcend vested interests and favor societal welfare as a whole. The styles and strategies of communication derived from such thinking could cultivate collaborative inquiry and a complexity of views and voices. Based on such broader conceptions of power and on the idea of a mutualism derived from *ubuntu*, I now turn to the formal properties of discourse and, in the next two chapters, begin the project of exploring and articulating a relational approach to public discourse as implied by *ubuntu*.

References

Amos, V. & Parmar, P. (1984). Challenging Imperial Feminism. *Feminist Review*, 17(1):3–19.

Arendt, H. (1969). *On Violence*. San Diego: Harvest.

Bahá'í International Community (2013). *Letter to the Bahá'ís in Iran*. A letter from the Bahá'í World Governing Body, 2 March 2013, Haifa, Israel.

Blankenberg, N. (1999). In Search of Real Freedom: Ubuntu and the Media. *Critical Arts*, 12(2):42–65.

Brocke-Utne, B. (1989). *Feminist Perspectives on Peace and Peace Education*. New York: Pergamon.

Boulding, K.E. (1990). *Three Faces of Power*. Newbury Park: Sage.

Bourdieu, P. (1994). Structures, Habitus, Power: Basis for a Theory of Symbolic Power. In Dirks, N.B., Eley, G. & Orthner, S.B. (eds). *Culture, Power, History: A Reader in Contemporary Social Theory*. Princeton: Princeton University Press.

Byrnes, R.M. (1996). *South Africa: A Country Study*. Washington: GPO for the Library of Congress.

Chasi, C. (2014). Violent Communication Is Not Alien to Ubuntu: Nothing Human Is Alien to Africans. *Communicatio: South African Journal for Communication Theory and Research*, 40(4):287–304.

Christians, C.G. (2004). Ubuntu and Communitarianism in Media Ethics. *Ecquid Novi*, 25(2):235–256.

Collins, P.H. (1990). *Black Feminist Thought: Knowledge, Consciousness, and the Politics of Empowerment*. Boston: Unwin Hyman.

Connolly, W. (1974). *The Terms of Political Discourse*. Lexington: Heath.

Crenshaw, K. (2015). *On Intersectionality: The Essential Writings of Kimberle Crenshaw*. New York: The New Press.

Dowding, K. (1996). *Power*. Milton Keynes: Open University Press.

Foucault, M. (1980). *Power/Knowledge*. Brighton: Harvester.

Giddens, A. (1984). *The Constitution of Society: Outline of the Theory of Structuration*. Cambridge: Polity Press.

Hartsock, N. (1983). *Money, Sex and Power: Towards a Feminist Historical Materialism*. New York: Longman.

Karlberg, M. (2002). Partisan Branding and Media Spectacle: Implications for Democratic Communication, *Democratic Communique*, 18:1–21.

Karlberg, M. (2004). *Beyond the Culture of Contest*. Oxford: George Ronald.

Karlberg, M. (2005). The Power of Discourse and the Discourse of Power: Pursuing Peace through Discourse Intervention. *International Journal of Peace Studies*, 10(1):1–25.

Lorde, A. (1984). *Age, Race, Class and Sex: Women Redefining Difference*. Berkeley: Crossing.

Louw, D.J. (2001). Ubuntu and the Challenge of Multiculturalism in Post-Apartheid South Africa, Unitwin Student Network, 2001, www.phys.uu.nl/~unitwin/, Accessed 4 November 2014.

Louw, D.J. (2010). Power Sharing and the Challenge of Ubuntu Ethics, Paper presented at the Forum for Religious Dialogue Symposium of the Research Institute for Theology and Religion at the University of South Africa, January 2010, Pretoria, South Africa.

Lukes, S. (1986). *Power*. New York: New York University Press.

Machiavelli, N. (1961). *The Prince*. London: Penguin.

Macpherson, C.B. (1973). *Democratic Theory: Essays in Retrieval*. Oxford: Oxford University Press.

Macquarrie, J. (1972). *Existentialism*. London: Penguin.

Metz, T. (2014). Harmonizing Global Ethics in the Future: A Proposal to Add South and East to West. *Journal of Global Ethics*, 10(2):146–155.

Metz, T. (2015). African Ethics and Journalism Ethics: News and Opinion in Light of Ubuntu. *Journal of Media Ethics: Exploring Questions of Media Morality*, 30(2):74–90.

Miller, J.B. (1982). Colloquium: Women and Power. *Stone Center for Developmental Services and Studies*, 82(1):1–5.

Moriarty, T.A. (2003). *Finding the Words: A Rhetorical History of South Africa's Transition from Apartheid to Democracy*. London: Praeger.

Moulton, J. (1983). A Paradigm of Philosophy: The Adversary Method. In Harding, S. & Hintikka, M. (eds) *Discovering Reality: Feminist Perspectives on Epistemology, Metaphysics, Methodology, and Philosophy of Science*. New York: Springer.

Nussbaum, M. (2011). *Creating Capabilities: The Human Development Approach*. Cambridge, MA: Belknap.

Parmar, P. (1990). *The Politics of Articulation in Identity: Community, Culture, Difference*. London: Lawrence & Wishart.

Ramsbotham, O. (2010). *Transforming Violent Conflict: Radical Disagreement, Dialogue and Survival*. London: Routledge.

Read, J.H. (2010). Leadership and Power in Nelson Mandela's Long Walk to Freedom. *Journal of Power*, 3(3):317–339.

Setiloane, G.M. (1993). Introduction. In Shutte, A. (ed). *Philosophy for Africa*. Cape Town: University of Cape Town Press.

Shutte, A. (1993). *Philosophy for Africa*. Cape Town: University of Cape Town Press.

Shutte, A. (2001). *Ubuntu: An Ethic for the New South Africa*. Cape Town: Cluster Publications.

Sommer, H. (1996). From Apartheid to Democracy: Patterns of Violent and Non-Violent Direct Action in South Africa 1984–1994. *Africa Today*, 43(1):53–76.

Swanson, D.M. (2012). Ubuntu, African Epistemology and Development: Contributions, Tensions, Contradictions and Possibilities. In Wright, H.K. & Abdi, A.A. (eds). *The Dialectics of African Education and Western Discourses: Appropriation, Ambivalence and Alternatives*: 27–52, New York: Peter Lang.

Tavernaro-Haidarian, L. (2016). Reality TV Has Had an Extreme Makeover in Soweto. Will It Work? *The Conversation*, 30 August 2017, https://theconversation.com/reality-tv-has-had-an-extreme-makeover-in-soweto-will-it-work-64084, Accessed 14 September 2017.

Tavernaro-Haidarian, L. (2018). Ubuntu and the Communication Power Nexus. In Mutsvairo, B. (ed). *Palgrave Handbook for Media and Communication Research in Africa*. London: Palgrave Macmillan.

Tolle, E. (2005). *A New Earth*. New York: Penguin.

Van Hensbroek, B. (1999). *Political Discourses in African Thought: 1960 to the Present*. Westport: Praeger.

Wartenberg, T.E. (1990). *The Forms of Power: From Domination to Transformation*. Philadelphia: Temple University Press.

Weber, M. (1986). Domination by Economic Power and by Authority. In Lukes, S. (ed). *Power*. New York: New York University Press.

Wrong, D.H. (1968). Some Problems in Defining Social Power. *American Journal of Sociology*, 73(6), 673–681.

3   Argument Culture

In comparison to the more affirmative or exploratory type of communication that usually emerges in interpersonal contexts, such as in conversations between friends and relatives where issues are considered from within one and the same camp and participants see each other as allies rather than opponents, the communication used in formal situations is frequently informed by conflictual notions of power, characterized by oppositional strategies and structured as an argument. Academic debates, where one challenges that which is offered by another, are one example of this dynamic and assume that in this way the best ideas and insights will inevitably emerge. Similarly, news programs, talk shows, reality television or public debates and discussions often cultivate an attitude of 'pro and con', 'right and wrong', 'black and white' or 'left and right', even if this occurs in polite and respectful ways and doubtlessly generates much knowledge and insight. In this chapter, however, I take a closer look at how restrictive some of these manifestations can be, how some of their formal properties could be informed by alternative strategies and how this can practically change the outcomes of communication.

Of course the question is why argumentative strategies, which typically fail in interpersonal situations and may even lead to estrangement or the breaking down of relations, are thought to be best in resolving issues or helping formulate collective plans in any other social context? The realism or 'deep frame' (Bateson, 1954) we continuously choose to operate from in the public sphere is premised on discord (Karlberg, 2004). As discussed in the previous chapters, this happens on an intrinsically cultural plain and is characterized by "moral and political principles that are so deep they are part of your very identity" (Lakoff, 2006:12). According to Lakoff, deep frames are like the foundational structures of our mind that shape our common sense and without which, "there is nothing for the surface message frames to hang on to" (ibid.). In the case of (mass-mediated) public discourse a deep frame may be thought of as adversarialism and a surface frame as the structural expressions of this, for example in terms of the formal properties of 'argument culture' (Tannen, 1998).

In argument culture discourses are structured as arguments. These can be understood as a "system of propositions linked by inference in order to persuade an audience on a controversial issue that a certain conclusion or set of conclusions is true and that some others are false" (Ramsbotham, 2010:38). This model "rests on the assumption that opposition is the best way to get anything done" (Tannen, 1998:3–4) and informs an approach where:

> Thinking of human interactions as battles is a metaphorical frame through which we learn to regard the world. The war on drugs, the war on cancer, the battle of the sexes, politicians' turf battles—in argument culture, war metaphors pervade our talk and shape our thinking. Nearly everything is framed as a battle or game in which winning and losing is the main concern.
>
> (Tannen, 1998:13)

First then, argument culture is characterized by a dichotomy or duality in which issues are represented and framed. In other words, two or more often stereotyped camps are articulated and matters are conceived of as mutually exclusive.

In daytime talk shows, for example, guests join a program and offer a specific position or view on the issue of the day. These positions are then confronted with opposing ones, as was the case in the battle between 'stay-at-home moms' and 'working moms' mentioned in the introduction. In her assessment of the above, Urban (2009:n.p.) explains that, although the episode touched on some important points, it was "rather polarizing and one-dimensional". Among her criticisms she mentions the lack of diversity among the talk show guests. For example, women who do part-time or shift-work or those who share the raising of their children with a spouse were missing from the conversation. She suggests that dads, employers, employment and child-care conditions (i.e. government policies) as well as the community at large also form important factors and are vital stakeholders in the raising of children—all of whom were absent from a discussion that featured only mothers who were at home all the time or those who worked outside of the home all the time (see Urban, 2009). This tug of war frame widens the chasm between parties and reduces the complexities of what is being discussed.

Of course frames, which contextualize and "suggest what the issue is through the use of selection, emphasis, exclusion and elaboration" (Tankard et al., 1991:5), are helpful in many ways as they assist us in focusing on what is relevant in any given context. Yet they can also be restrictive, particularly when we are unaware of the deeper assumptions they entail. For example, an issue that is generally thought of as controversial and is often framed in binary ways is abortion. This multi-faceted and highly sensitive topic that affects women's autonomy as well as society's interest in protecting fetal life is usually framed as 'pro choice' versus 'pro life' but has also been framed in terms of assessing which is more important: women's privacy or universal morality? (see Mollmann, 2012). In this context, Mollmann (ibid.:n.p.) suggests that this kind of framing is dangerous as "universal morality would appear to be a broader and more applicable common good than guaranteeing the right of a handful of women to a specific medical procedure because of concern for their private lives". In this either/or scenario the possible common sense conclusions are limited by their very framing and enable the favoring of one over the other. Yet, as she notes, it is possible to question this framing and to reconsider the generalized notion of privacy to include instead the idea of women's ability to realize their full potential. In other words, "when a government unduly limits access to a medical procedure only women need, it not only infringes on their privacy, it engages in blatant discrimination" (ibid.)—something that can be considered to be as weighty as 'universal morality'. So changing the frame changes what is at stake. Of course it is possible, in turn, to dissect and reframe Mollmann's statement and to consider why women might 'need' this procedure in the first place; what the complex socio-political, ethical and values-based realities are that give rise to this need and of course what overarching societal changes could or should be considered in preventing this need before it grows into one.

In all these ways, then, it is possible to realize how limiting and yet how important framing can be and that being conscious of frames, considering multiple frames and striving for open-ended framing can all be effective ways of ensuring that we engage with discourses in more complete ways and that we open up a number of possible solutions.

In view of the wealth of insights that can open up when frames do, pushing one particular view or stance becomes prohibitive. Here it is possible to question the second feature of argument culture, namely its primarily persuasive approach to rhetoric (see Tannen, 1998:13), which is firmly anchored in our dominant ethico-cultural realism. In the same way that theorists of power are primarily occupied with domination, persuasion seems to be the central understanding in rhetorical theory. From Aristotle (Freese, 1982) to Habermas (1984) and Dahlgren (1995), the idea that persuasion is the primary focus of any rhetorical exercise prevails (see also Asante, 1990; Shepherd, 1992). This understanding is one in which the rhetor has the power to persuade others, an audience or a jury of the validity of her argument and to win it so to speak.

This can be done through rational and logical appeals or by drumming up emotions. For example, Fisher (1987:71) contrasts the 'rational-world paradigm', where "clear-cut inferential or implicative structures" are the currency for participating in discourse, with the 'narrative paradigm'. This model is distinguished "by the nature of persons as narrative beings", which renders everyone qualified to make sense of and participate in public discourses based on their ability to measure those discourses against their own inherent compass (ibid.:72). According to Fisher, we organize the world in terms of the narratives we have internalized and continue to live out. The more coherence and fidelity a person's story or a situation has with those narratives, the more powerful they become in influencing our decision-making. This is particularly true for our current political climate. In what is frequently referred to as the post-truth era, where appeals to emotion take precedence over factual accuracy, truth is often sidelined in favor of an alignment with internal narratives. As a result, polarization along narrative lines has become the defining feature of 21st-century politics (see Doherty, 2014). Such practices are not limited to the realm of governance and can also be evidenced throughout the media landscape, where products, services, medicines and political parties are also packaged to evoke feelings of trust, quality and longevity and to attract customers, clients and members. Most advertisements, for example, focus less on the factual content of what they are selling than on the emotional brand they are creating.

This is not necessarily bad. Persuasion can save lives if it prevents someone from jumping off a bridge. So it is possible to acknowledge that persuasion is a vital element of communication and one that I very much employ in this book to present new and under-developed ideas. However, my aim is also to 'explore' such ideas, which is a function of communication that does not feature as prominently in the scholarship on rhetoric. Here, the concept of 'invitational rhetoric' (Foss & Griffin, 1997) stands out and reminds us that there can be an alternative aim. Invitational rhetoric is based on the idea that themes can be explored collectively and with a degree of detachment or distance from one's own view. Rhetors need not "seek to impose their position on audience members", rather, they can "give voice" to a (one of many) perspectives (Foss & Griffin, 1997:118).

In this vein, it is possible to apply a more integrative view that includes both approaches by proposing a distinction between the primary objective of a rhetorical exercise and its secondary objective or not necessarily intended outcome. In other words, it is indeed possible to embark on a communicative act that is meant to be invitational or exploratory rather than persuasive, even if this process has some persuasive outcomes. Both features can play a role. In fact, such mixed dynamics inform all forms of negotiation, dialogue or deliberation, as was the case during the public deliberations that helped shape and provide feedback to South Africa's first constitution (see Salazar, 2002:93). Exploration is a vital and ubiquitous element of communication and one that deserves attention.

The concept of invitational rhetoric, then, helps shift the primary focus away from the need to win an argument and toward a desire to earnestly explore the various facets of a subject. It foregrounds exploration and backgrounds persuasion. In this way, power inequalities related to the ability of certain rhetors to be particularly eloquent or knowledgeable become less material as does the need to substitute this ability with narrative or emotional prowess. This creates a more equal playing field for people of all backgrounds and interests.

Such expanded notions of rhetoric and framing need not play out in theory alone. Practical examples prevail. A comparative analysis of two daytime talk shows I sampled in 2017, one from the United States and one from South Africa, reveals some of the contrasting ways in which topics can be framed and rhetoric employed (see Tavernaro-Haidarian, 2017). In this study, I looked at how the topics of 'teen pregnancy' and 'teen marriage' were treated differently across four talk show episodes in the last decade, specifically as regards framing and rhetoric but also in terms of how identity was treated and mediation was facilitated. Because a detailed treatment of the case studies exceeds the scope of this project, I provide only a brief summary that reveals how and to what effect these formal properties played out in practice:

Case Study 1

In the first case study from the United States, topics were framed in binaries that offered an either/or view of the issues discussed. Teen pregnancy was framed as an 'epidemic' with those who were there to challenge it and those who were there to defend it. Similarly, through the introduction of the topic and of individual guests, the subject of teen marriage was framed as an act that occurred 'too soon', with those whose agenda it was to defend this position and those who questioned it. The lines of action implied in the above approach are limited as participants of the discourse can only chose to consent or oppose the constructed framing with very little room for exploring the complexities and subtleties that may emanate from individual circumstance, culture or belief. This type of surface framing reveals the nature of the adversarial realism that informs it and also contributes to the unconscious assumption that conflict is a natural way to organize affairs (see Karlberg, 2004). Where complexities and subtleties came to the fore, the host brought the discussion back to the original framing, thereby confining the scope of communication to the outcomes implied in that framing. This contributed to "reconstituting the world in similar ways" (Dunwoody & Griffin, 1993:24) rather than exploring the possibilities of alternative truths informed by the situations, values and realities of those present in the discussion.

The primary focus of the host's rhetoric was to persuade guests "that a certain conclusion or set of conclusions is true and that some others are false" (Ramsbotham, 2010:38). She pushed the dominant view that getting married 'too soon' and having children as teenagers was wrong, while her teenage guests defended theirs. There was very little "re-sourcement [. . .], which involves deploying another logic or system" (Foss & Griffin, 1997:7) as the framing limited the rhetorical freedom of participants. Some overtly hurtful and confrontational statements were also made, particularly by the host (e.g. "Ya'll are dumb"). She used all three kinds of persuasive appeal that Aristotle refers to (see Freese, 1982:45). Namely, appeals to the *logos* (logic), as she cited reasons for the intellectual inferiority of her guests; appeals to the *pathos* (emotions) as she called on the guest's often crying family members to persuade their loved ones out of having children or getting married; and appeals to the *ethos* (the character or credibility of the rhetor), as she quizzed her young guests on questions of income and expenditure, which they were unable to answer. The main objectives of her rhetoric were to offer praise or blame of her guests and to persuade the audience to judge their future or past actions. When talk show guests listened to each other this was done primarily to identify flaws in the arguments of those they were talking with and to formulate a response or rebuttal, often acknowledged with a round of applause by the audience. This affirmed one camp's point of view and discouraged an earnest quest into understanding or at least growing in their understanding of the other.

With the aim being to win an argument, each guest was also strongly identified with the constructed 'us' at the expense of 'them', which is one prevalent way in which identity is constructed (see Burke, 1969). As such, the identities of the host and her guests were formed oppositionally and were mostly fixed to a single position, rather than fluid. Talk show guests spent their energies defending their positions rather than seeking to understand or bridge their views (see Burke, 1969).

The host deepened this divide by humiliating or challenging her guests and ridiculing their answers, as she did when one of her guests did not know the definition of the word 'quintuplets'. The audience frequently laughed or clapped with her, thus reinforcing her interpretation or stance on a given topic and entrenching the camps. The host also reiterated or laundry aired her guest's positions and personal circumstances in repetitive ways, thereby reinforcing the shock value of their unusual choices.

Overall, while mostly warm and empathetic in tone (though arguably patronizing in the process), the first case study offered more of an adversarial spectacle than a collective inquiry and emphasized conflict over common ground. It employed exclusionary framing, a chiefly persuasive rhetorical approach, fostered conflictual identities among participants and cultivated a rather authoritarian form of mediation.

Case Study 2

In the second case study from South Africa, the framing of the topic was comparatively open-ended. Specifically, the title and introduction of the topics by the host, ('Teen Pregnancy' and 'Right Time to Marry') implied rather infinite lines of action as participants of the discourse were able to explore 'when' the right time to marry could be and 'what' teen pregnancy may entail for the life of an individual, family or community. Thus, the framing encouraged contrasting and complementary views and allowed for the relativity that comes with individual circumstance, context, culture or belief. This implies a level of respect for and cultivation of diversity. The discussion in these episodes also presented many contrasting yet not conflicting angles and viewpoints. In this regard, difference was framed or perceived as complementarity rather than divergence. Both the guests and the host allowed each other the time and space to complete their thoughts and often agreed with each other's points while offering alternative views based on their individual experiences. In cases where they disagreed, they frequently did so by validating the statements made before them (with phrases such as "That is true, but from my experience") and then elaborating accordingly. As such, a potentially unlimited range of nuances and complexities could be safely explored and diverse insights encouraged. Moreover, the individual introduction of the guests occurred in a way that did not delineate any clear camps. Rather, guests were there to collectively share their experiences and to consider each other's views on the topic. They were also more diverse in their experiential backgrounds than the guests in the first case study and included a wider range of community members, which indicates consciousness of the broader discursive context. The framing was thus telling of a more deliberative or mutualistic approach to communication and a participatory worldview in which reality is seen as somewhat relative.

The rhetorical focus of both the guests and the host was to each offer perspectives and personal experiences with the aim of exploring matters collectively. Guests made frequent "leaps to the other side", which let them "deploy another logic or system" (Foss & Griffin, 1997:9) and sympathize with and even agree with another's point of view. For example, while trying to explore ways of curbing teen pregnancy, one of the guests (a high school teacher) made references to the many underlying reasons she felt teenagers fell pregnant, thereby identifying with her student's personal circumstances. She explored these together with the teenage guest in non-threatening ways and without accusations or criticism. In their conversation, they did not oppose each other but rather invited each other to help uncover the underlying motives and needs of teenagers. Thus, the rhetorical approach became "an invitation to understanding as a means to create a relationship rooted in equality, immanent value and self-determination" (Foss & Griffin, 1997:5). This opened common ground from which participants were able to probe and clarify underlying ideas. Conflict was dissipated by unifying statements such as when one guest said, "All of these reasons are true, of course"; by disclaimers, for example when guests would say "But from my experience"; and by frequent acknowledgments of participant's contributions in the form of "Thank you for that". By using phrases such as "From my perspective" the rhetors provided a context for their views, as they expressed and made space for multiple interpretations and cultural complexities in order to gain more insight into each other's perspective (see Christians, 2004). This was conducive of collaboration and "offered friendliness where friendliness is given" (Metz, 2015:340). By affording each other ample time to complete thoughts and statements, the participants cultivated an 'ethic of listening' and looked for ways in which their narratives were "connected, interrelated and interdependent" (Wasserman, 2013:78–79). This was not a mere toleration of ideas but rather an effort to identify with one another, to "strain to hear" (Foss & Griffin, 1997:13) as when the host repeatedly probed and clarified what her younger guest was thinking and feeling rather than making assumptions. This created respect as all participants had the right to share and to be "heard into being" (Foss & Griffin, 1997:11).

Guests were also able to share one another's points of view by completing each other's sentences. In other words, the identities of the talk show guests were not fixed to a single position but rather fluid, implying a relational conception of power. Participants seemed to identify themselves with a greater 'we' that included their fluid and nested sub-identities as women, mothers, daughters or social workers. This was emphasized by the frequent use of the word 'we' where, for example, one guest (an educational psychologist) suggested that "We (i.e. the community or society) have to address the issue together". Talk show guests thus conceived of or rather experienced their "beliefs as beliefs that they" were "holding" rather than "beliefs" that had "them in their hold" (Louw, 2001:21). This points to a level of detachment from positionality or positional statements.

This detachment and self-reflexivity was apparent in more direct ways when, for example, the host ruminated on her inability to get young men to participate in the discussion on pregnancy. Hence, the mediator was part of the bigger 'we' and it became "a process of learning for both facilitator and participant" (Blankenberg, 1999:46). Her own views were woven in as they became experientially relevant, for example when she mentioned her insights as a mother of twins. In contrast to the first case study, the host did not clearly identify or articulate a single or dominant position, offering mostly questions rather than opinions. Where humor was introduced, the host laughed with her guests instead of at them. Unlike the more hurtful and divisive tone of humor or ridicule that emerged in the first case study, the humor here provided moments of comic relief and a sense of togetherness as guests and a viewer who had called in laughed about a comical situation in the absence of a studio audience. The host frequently raised the discussion to the level of principle rather than focusing on the personal or shocking details of her guest's experiences, and concluded her episodes with information that empowered viewers to make up their own minds about the choices they make in their lives instead of summing up her view of the right approach. This is in line with the *ubuntu* conception of humanness, which denotes "to belong and to participate" (Mkhize, 2008:39–40).

Overall, the discussion in the second case study was both dialogical (see Briand, 1995), in that it was informal and provided a framework for exchanging diverse perspectives and considering various values, as well as more instrumental and deliberative (see Dillon, 1994), as the discussion sometimes became focused to accommodate recommendations for viewers and callers. It employed open-ended framing, a chiefly exploratory rhetorical approach, fostered a 'we' identity among participants and cultivated a facilitatory form of mediation.

While the second case study is certainly revealing of alternative cultural sensibilities in the South African context, not all programs emerging from South Africa play out in this way. Similarly, such relational approaches are not entirely absent in the United States or in other places around the world. One emerging US talk show for example, "where masculinity is redefined and men can open up about emotions and manhood", is being described as a "disruptive weekly panel series" (Wagmeister, 2017:n.p.), in which cultural norms are challenged and issues relating to men are discussed in non-threatening and exploratory ways. Acknowledging the potential need to first cultivate a taste for such programs, the show's own producer proposes that,

> Our intention for creating this show is not just to be seen by millions, but to be seen by the people who need it, who are ready for it [. . .] it's about the integrity of the conversation, and the intention behind the show.
>
> (Baldoni in Wagmeister, 2017:n.p.)

In other words, public conversations do not always have to pan out in oppositional and persuasive ways.

Yet whether such examples can ultimately withstand the force of profit motives that have hinged for so long on shock and spectacle becomes a question of nurturing alternative tastes over time. Governed by a market logic that results "in the stratification of audiences according to income and social position" (Wasserman, 2013:72), commercial media houses are constantly looking for ways in which to stay in the game and this is achieved, in part, by providing a constant stream of escalated conflict and controversy. In this context, public and community media provide a level of relief but do not paradigmatically transcend a normative culture of adversarialism or argument culture. Usually they provide elevated, refined and intelligent versions of the same.

And while a level of conflict and confrontation may appear harmless in entertainment based contexts, where the aim is to have some fun, the underlying messages and assumptions are not as innocuous as their intentions may be. As the above case study suggests, talks shows can exert a subtle yet powerful role in normalizing adversarial approaches to culture and continue to nurture these sensitivities within new generations of both consumers and producers of the media. As a result, it becomes self-evident to apply argument culture in many contexts such as in social, scientific, economic, judicial and governance related settings, where alternative approaches could in fact make a significant difference and lead to more complex insights and to increasingly sustainable solutions for larger portions of society.

Of course from within the unconscious realism of a society inundated by argument culture, non-adversarial models of communication and social interaction may appear unsophisticated and idealistic. In this regard, normative adversarialism can be seen as a somewhat 'hegemonic' cultural formation (Karlberg, 2004:79) in which the interests of a vast majority are sidelined and argumentation appears to be the only natural and inevitable form of communication. It is perhaps from within this standpoint, too, that criticisms have been directed at the talk show in the second case study mentioned above, which, though running for over 12 years and winning numerous awards, has also been described as not being engaging enough (see Tavernaro-Haidarian, 2017:315). It is often difficult to rise above the schemes and patterns we've grown comfortable with. Yet it is not impossible. In light of the ultimate fluidity of culture and ethics (see Kehoe, 1992) and in view of the above-mentioned case study, which employed collaborative and deliberative communication strategies and captured audiences for over a decade, it is clear that alternatives are always possible. In the next chapter I bring such an approach into clearer focus by contrasting the constituent elements of argument culture with elements informed by the normative moral theory of *ubuntu* and by articulating more fully the idea of 'deliberation culture'.

References

Asante, M.K. (1990). *Kemet, Afrocentricity and Knowledge*. Trenton: Africa World Press.

Bateson, G. (1954). A Theory of Play and Fantasy. In Bateson, G. (ed). *Steps to an Ecology of Mind*: 177–193, New York: Ballantine.

Blankenberg, N. (1999). In Search of Real Freedom: Ubuntu and the Media. *Critical Arts*, 12(2):42–65.

Briand, M. (1995). *Building Deliberative Communities*. Charlottesville: Pew Partnerships for Civic Change.

Burke, K. (1969). *A Rhetoric of Motives*. Berkeley: University of California Press.

Christians, C.G. (2004). Ubuntu and Communitarianism in Media Ethics. *Ecquid Novi*, 25(2):235–256.

Dahlgren, P. (1995). *Television and the Public Sphere: Citizenship, Democracy and the Media*. London: Sage.

Dillon, J.T. (1994). *Deliberation in Education and Society*. Norwood: Ablex Publishing Corporation.

Doherty, C. (2014). 7 Things to Know about Polarization in America, Pew Research Center, 12 June 2014, www.pewresearch.org/fact-tank/2014/06/12/7-things-to-know-about-polarization-in-america/, Accessed 12 September 2017.

Dunwoody, S. & Griffin, R. (1993). Journalistic Strategies for Reporting Long-Term Environmental Issues: A Case Study of Three Superfund Sites. In Hansen, A. (ed). *The Mass Media and Environmental Issues*. London: Leicester University Press.

Fisher, W.R. (1987). *Human Communication as Narration: Toward a Philosophy of Reason, Value and Action*. Columbia: University of South Carolina Press.

Foss, S. & Griffin, C. (1997). Transforming Rhetoric through Feminist Reconstruction: A Response to the Gender Diversity Perspective. *Women's Studies in Communication*, 20(2):117–135.

Freese, J.H. (1982). *The Art of Rhetoric*. Cambridge: Harvard University Press.

Habermas, J. (1984). *Moral Consciousness and Communicative Action*. Boston: Beacon.

Karlberg, M. (1997). News and Conflict: How Adversarial News Frames Limit Public Understanding of Environmental Issues. *Alternatives Journal*, 23(1):33–48.

Karlberg, M. (2004). *Beyond the Culture of Contest*. Oxford: George Ronald.

Kehoe, A. (1992). Conflict Is a Western Worldview. In Rohrl, V., Nicolson, M. & Zamora, M. (eds). *The Anthropology of Peace*: 55–66, Williamsburg: Studies in Third World Societies.

Lakoff, G. (2006). *Whose Freedom? The Battle over America's Most Important Idea*. New York: Farrar, Straus & Giroux.

Louw, D.J. (2001). Ubuntu and the Challenge of Multiculturalism in Post-Apartheid South Africa, Unitwin Student Network, www.phys.uu.nl/~unitwin/, Accessed 4 November 2014.

Metz, T. (2015). African Ethics and Journalism Ethics: News and Opinion in Light of Ubuntu. *Journal of Media Ethics: Exploring Questions of Media Morality*, 30(2):74–90.

Mkhize, N. (2008). Ubuntu and Harmony: An African Approach to Morality and Ethics. In Nicolson, R. (ed). *Persons in Community: African Ethics in a Global Culture*: 35–44, Pietermaritzburg: University of KwaZulu-Natal Press.

Mollmann, M. (2012). The Problematic Framing of Abortion as an Issue of Privacy. *The Huffington Post*, 24 March 2012, www.huffingtonpost.com/marianne-mollmann/the-problematic-framing-o_b_1222528.html, Accessed 7 August 2017.

Ramsbotham, O. (2010). *Transforming Violent Conflict: Radical Disagreement, Dialogue and Survival*. London: Routledge.

Salazar, P.J. (2002). *An African Athens: Rhetoric and the Shaping of Democracy in South Africa*. Mahwah: Lawrence Erlbaum.

Shepherd, G.J. (1992). Communication as Influence: Definitional Exclusion. *Communication Studies*, 43(1):203–219.

Tankard, J.W., Hendrickson, L., Silberman, J., Bliss, K. & Chanem, S. (1991). Media Frames: Approaches to Conceptualization and Measurement, Paper presented at the Association for Education in Journalism and Mass Communication Annual Meeting, August 1991, Boston, MA, USA.

Tannen, D. (1998). *The Argument Culture*. New York: Random House.

Tavernaro-Haidarian, L. (2017). Talking Ubuntu: Toward a Relational Talk Show Model, Doctoral Dissertation, University of Johannesburg.

Urban, A. (2009). Dr. Phil Stay-at-Home Mom vs. Working Mom Show, PhD in Parenting, 14 October 2009, www.phdinparenting.com/blog/2009/10/14/dr-phil-stay-at-home-mom-vs-working-mom-show.html, Accessed 7 August 2017.

Wagmeister, E. (2017). 'Jane the Virgin' Star Justin Baldoni Developing Men's Talk Show. *Variety*, 6 July 2017, http://variety.com/2017/tv/news/justin-baldoni-talk-show-the-mens-room-1202488304/, Accessed 8 August 2017.

Wasserman, H. (2013). Journalism in a New Democracy: The Ethics of Listening. *Communicatio: South African Journal for Communication Theory and Research*, 39(1):67–84.

4   Deliberation Culture

Discourses and discursive processes do not exist in a vacuum. They are molded by the broader values that envelop them and, in turn, they continue to influence those broader values. They can also be deconstructed to reveal the variable projection of meanings and messages embedded in them as well as the assumptions implicit in them (Derrida, 1967). Reconsidering the strategies of 'argument culture' (Tannen, 1998) specifically helps us reimagine how we could be thinking, talking and relating to one another in ways that are relational rather than conflictual. This is my project in the present chapter, where I refer to the formal properties of this approach and discuss how these would crystalize differently if they were informed by the African philosophy of *ubuntu*. By drawing on the scholarship on *ubuntu* and on other relevant theories and examples, I tease out the features of a model of public discourse, which I call 'deliberation culture' and which derives from deeply relational values.

Relationality in African thought has most often been interpreted "in terms of harmony" (Metz, 2014a:148), where the wellbeing of every member relies on the wellbeing of the social body as a whole. It is constituted by a "web of relations free of friction and conflict" (Masolo, 2010:24) though rich in even paradoxical perspectives. Power lies in uniting "different beings [. . .], without confusing them" (Blankenberg, 1999:43) and "enables each individual to become a unique center of shared life" (Shutte, 2001:9). Such is the basis of the idea of deliberation culture, which constitutes a contribution to the scholarship that is forming around various expressions of mutualism (see Bahá'í International Community, 1995; Emmet, 2009; Karlberg, 2004; Kolstoe, 1990). In order to conceptualize it more fully, I want to motivate the term 'deliberation' further. I began this effort in the introductory chapter, which clarified that the word is to be associated more closely with the mutualistic approach of traditional African practices (see

Blankenberg, 1999) rather than the ideals of deliberative democracy, which can still assume agonistic worldviews and cultivate persuasion.

Building on this idea and in contrast to more conflictual strategies, such as debates and arguments, where "victory usually goes to he who can catch the other in more contradictions" (Galtung, 2004:38), communication within the broadly relational spectrum can also be said to be more or less 'dialogical' or 'deliberative' (Karlberg, 2004:112). In "A dialogue [. . .] there is no competition to win a battle of words" (Galtung, 2004:38). Dialogue can be seen as a more exploratory process, where parties exchange ideas and views with the aim of gaining more insight into an issue and broadening their own horizons (see Briand, 1995; Bridges, 1994; Dillon, 1994). Deliberation, in turn, is often understood as employing the principles of dialogue but for the more instrumental purpose of arriving at a specific decision or delineating a specific course of action (Karlberg, 2004:112). Therefore, the idea of deliberation expresses agency, which can channel the co-created power of those engaged in the communicative process toward a common goal, such as a decision, a plan of action or any other advisory or executive outcome. In view of the above and with the objectives traditionally associated with *ubuntu*, where communities meet up for the instrumental purpose of decision-making, the more dynamic notion of 'deliberation culture' rather than 'dialogue culture' becomes relevant as an alternative to argument culture. This does not mean that such communicative processes must always be deliberative. They can exhibit more or less dialogical or deliberative outcomes. However, broadly, they can be associated with the problem-solving focus that characterizes traditional community meetings as well as democratic processes or mediated contexts more generally.

In order to clarify how deliberation culture might achieve these objectives, it is useful to consider its constituent elements in terms of framing and rhetoric as suggested in the previous chapter. However, the discussion in Chapter 3 also revealed that identity and mediation are relevant and constitutive of processes associated with public discourse. For this reason, I now consider all of these variables in light of the realism that *ubuntu* provides:

Framing

As a "central organizing idea [. . .] that supplies context" (Tankard et al., 1991:5) the framing associated with deliberation culture facilitates "a more inclusive way [of] reporting on issues" (Rodny-Gumede, 2015:112) than argument culture does, one that is deeply participatory.

To delve into a practical example, it is possible to consider what is known as the 2012 'Marikana massacre' in South Africa, in which South African security forces used lethal force against striking civilian mine workers in the Marikana area of the country. Rodny-Gumede (2015) describes how news networks relied heavily on embedded journalism and consulted government, police and mining sources who all had a vested interest in curbing the very legitimate grievances of protesting miners. This prevented South African journalists from including a wider span of sources and perspectives. She reflects on the reporting of this event through the lens of 'peace journalism', a theory of the press derived from *ubuntu*, and argues that an *ubuntu*-based approach to the coverage could have mitigated the sensationalism and polarization that emerged in the news.

In deliberation culture, then, framing pans out in an inclusive and open-ended manner and in terms of complementary rather than mutually exclusive perspectives. Frames are constructed as a means of enabling as diverse a range of insights, angles and viewpoints as contextually possible so that a fuller picture can emerge. For example, instead of framing parenting discourses as battles between 'working moms' and 'stay-at-home moms', they can be reframed in a more open-ended manner, namely as inquiries into 'how we can mine the gems in children'. This invites a richness of perspectives, enhanced by guests whose experiences span a broad range of backgrounds in relation to raising children. While this is one of any number of ways in which a narrower frame can be opened up, transcending argument culture in this context means offering at least more than two ways of contextualizing an issue. Thus, communicators essentially constitute panelists of one and the same side, exploring those frames from a variety of experiential viewpoints. This variety and diversity of narratives is a basic premise of complementarity. And if narrative is "a basic feature of human action [. . .] [then] to deny value to another's capacity for narrative—to deny her potential for voice— is to deny a basic dimension of human life" (Couldry, 2010:1). Opening up frames enables more narratives to enter discursive processes. Open and complementary frames help us look for "ways in which our narratives are connected, interrelated and interdependent" (Wasserman, 2013:78). Each individual narrative is seen as part of an "interlocking set of narratives" (Couldry, 2010:8). These have to be spoken and heard. "To have something to say is to be a person. But speaking depends on listening and being heard; it is an intensely relational act" (Gilligan, 1993:xiii). Therefore framing in deliberation culture aims to maximize rather than limit diversity of thought and its resulting lines of action.

To apply this approach on another example from the media, it is possible to consider Kelly's (2013) account of the reporting around the shooting of a United States Congresswoman in 2011. She relays the media's framing of the gunman's motives as a mutually exclusive battle between his mental health and the influence political vitriol had on him. Kelly (2013:3–4) quotes the media in a headline that states, "As portrait of [the gunman] sharpens, vitriol blames fade!" and proposes that the "binary frame is apparent in the verbal pairing of 'sharpens/fades', with the implication that there is only a fixed amount of energy that can be distributed across these two causal forces". By contrast, if one were to frame this issue from a posture of deliberation culture, the following sample statement could be made: "Various factors may have contributed to the gunman's act of violence. These include his damaged mental health and a political climate that contributed to hateful images of the Congresswoman". Note the implied 'or' is replaced by 'and'.

Another headline is quoted by Kelly (2013:4) that reads: "Emerging information about [the] primary suspect [. . .] suggests that he was motivated not by a climate of hate but rather by his own troubled mind" thus, both "the introduction and the juxtaposition of 'not by/but rather' constructs a zero-sum binary frame, with vitriol clearly on the 'losing' side". Kelly suggests that the framing implicitly justifies decreasing coverage of the hostility that dominated the political climate leading up to the attack. Reworking this frame in line with a relational understanding of human affairs could look something like this: "Emerging information about the primary suspect suggests that he was motivated both by a climate of hate and a troubled mind", or "Emerging information about the primary suspect suggests he could have been motivated by a variety of issues, including a climate of hate and a troubled mind".

A third example is a caption that accompanied the gunman's mug shot: "Does the grin convey a sense of accomplishment or complete disengagement from the consequences of his actions?" (Kelly, 2013:4). This question implies that his sense of accomplishment and his insanity are two, mutually exclusive possibilities. According to Kelly, this obscures many other angles such as the effect hate speech and political vitriol may have on mental illness or how the two interact. Of course it is possible to raise many other alarming concerns about the framing of a story that involves a White gunman and characterizes his motives in terms of mental instability rather than the possibility of a terrorist act for example. Fairclough (2003) refers to this process as 'bracketing'. Bracketing can be understood as a form of 'elite continuity' (see Wasserman, 2013) insofar as the media favors those voices that are often aligned with positions of authority over others, eclipsing entire facets or possibilities of reality. A piece on the same issue exhibiting deliberation culture might include both the perpetrator's feeling of achievement and his detachment from his actions as two (of many) possible and possibly interacting factors in what the author would 'authentically disclose' (see Christians, 2004) as his personal reading of a mug shot. In other words, media professionals would find ways of contextualizing their view as one of many in an ongoing discourse. This would pan out as a joint collaboration between researchers, specialists, commentators and ordinary citizens who have a perspective to offer on "how different causal forces [. . .] might interact and interrelate" (Kelly, 2013:5) and has vast implications for all spheres of public life, including law and justice.

Another befitting example of how a narrow frame can be opened up involves the 'police versus public' binary associated with police violence in the United States. Here, comedian Trevor Noah (2015:n.p.) suggests that,

> We live in world where policing is frequently the symptom not the cause of the inequality. It can't be that police are on the one side and the community is on the other. The police are the public and the public is the police.

By merging the police-force with the concept of the public/community, Noah breaks the binary of police versus the public and challenges his viewers to explore their own biases and acknowledge their own role in the creation of an environment and society where police crimes can happen.

In a deliberative approach to public discourse based in *ubuntu*, then, framing is open to bringing together differing, even clashing, perspectives that invite the overlapping and interrelating of ideas so that citizens can craft collective responses that are well informed and benefit the community at large.

Rhetoric

A model of public discourse, which invites the overlapping and interrelating of ideas, also employs a chiefly 'invitational' (Foss & Griffin, 1997) or exploratory rather than persuasive rhetorical approach. This is not to disregard the role of persuasion in communication, which is absolutely central to the human experience.

In this vein, Moriarty (2003:323) relays the significance of Nelson Mandela's deliberative persuasion skills in communicating with both defenders and opponents of the *apartheid* regime who demanded a victory on the battlefield rather than the negotiating table: "Mandela had to persuade all sides to 'envision' racial power relations in variable-sum rather than zero-sum terms". Since all sides were still operating from a zero-sum discursive or conceptual universe, where racial power relations were conceived of as conflicting, Mandela's job was to persuade all sides to buy into a variable-sum vision of power relations—or relational power. Once this was achieved, negotiations could take place. In other words, persuasion is a key element in discourses that presume 'power over' or conflicts of power. That is why, when operating from within a discursive reality that naturalizes conflict, persuasion becomes instrumental of argument culture.

However, it is possible to consider that, from an alternative discursive reality, one of harmony, cohesion and *ubuntu*, where relational conceptions of power are the accepted framework, focusing on other aspects of rhetoric can be more effective. In this alternative discursive reality, participants of a discourse buy into their inherent oneness, even if, or precisely because, this oneness presumes diversity. In the *ubuntu* conception of human relations, one's humanity allows diverse individuals to ascend their various individual positions in order to become congruous. Thus, the approach to rhetoric most effective for deliberation culture and its relational understanding of power may be primarily invitational. In an increasingly diverse, complex and interconnected world, "rather than persuasion, rhetoric could be an invitation to understanding as a means to create a relationship rooted in equality, immanent value and self-determination" (Foss & Griffin, 1997:5). Here the term 'equality' suggests that all participants have something to gain from cooperating in the rhetorical exercise. And while invitational rhetoric is merely one of many forms of rhetoric not advocated in all situations (see ibid.), in the context of deliberation culture, the ability of invitational rhetoric to offer ideas and perspectives without necessarily imposing a position on others but rather by giving voice to a perspective becomes particularly relevant.

This is in line with the *ubuntu* conception of humanness, which implies "to belong and to participate" (Mkhize, 2008:39–40). When rhetors offer their perspectives, they do so "not to gain adherence to that view, but rather, to enhance their understanding of it" (Bone et al., 2008:436). "Rhetors must be willing to yield, which involves a turning toward the other [. . .] meeting another's position in its uniqueness, letting it have it impact" (Foss & Griffin, 1997:7). For this to happen communicators must be willing to "risk themselves in exchanges and call into question the beliefs they consider most inviolate and relax their grip on those beliefs" (ibid.). Meeting another's position and risking self is a requirement of *ubuntu*'s prescription to identify and exhibit solidarity with others in order to "become a real person or to realize one's true self" (Metz, 2011; Metz & Gaie, 2010; Mnyaka & Motlhabi, 2005). One way to do this is to offer 're-sourcement' which involves making a "swerve, a leap to the other side, which lets us [. . .] deploy another logic or system" (Foss & Griffin, 1997:9). This ties in with the idea that, in *ubuntu*, participants of a discourse express and disclose multiple interpretations and cultural complexities in order to gain more insight into each perspective (see Christians, 2004). As Deutsch (2000:32,35) suggests:

> When there is disagreement, seek to understand the other's views from his or her perspective; try to feel what it would be like if you were on the other side. [. . .] Reasonable people understand that their own judgment as well as the judgment of others may be fallible.

The external conditions that are required for such an approach, according to Foss and Griffin (1997:10), are those of safety, value and freedom. Safety involves "creating a feeling of security" for communicators to know that "ideas and feelings will not be denigrated or trivialized" through others. This requires participants of an *ubuntu-inspired* discourse to exhibit humanness insofar as this means "you are generous [. . .] hospitable [. . .] friendly and caring and compassionate" (Tutu, 1999:31).

Value is the "acknowledgment that audience members have intrinsic or immanent worth" (Foss & Griffin, 1997:11). In other words, as in *ubuntu*, they are truly valued, enjoy freedom of expression and are "not limited to what elders find agreeable" (Chasi, 2014a). True to *ubuntu*, the individual is treated "as special in virtue of her capacity to enter into relationships of identity and solidarity" (Metz, 2015:78). So for deliberation culture this means that the views of others are seen as inherently valuable regardless of their age, social position or level of education. For this to happen communicators have to be willing to depart from their own worldview and to strive to understand or hear the other, which means cultivating an 'ethic of listening' (see Wasserman, 2013). In Wasserman's (2013:78–79) approach, participants of a discourse "look for ways in which" their "narratives are connected, interrelated and interdependent". This is particularly important for instances where listening is difficult, tedious or challenging as it requires those engaged in a discourse to cultivate this capacity. As Bickford (1996:13) proposes, "listening does not mean mere toleration of another's utterance but rather an effort" to identify with another and "to strain to hear what common purpose or common good may be shared among people across their differences". This requires effort (Wasserman, 2013:80). In this context, moral reasoning evolves "because people are able to share one another's point of view in the social situation" (Denzin, 1997:277).

In order to highlight the practical efficacy of this approach, Bone et al. (2008:453) relay how a public conversations project designed to bring together people on 'both sides' of the abortion debate benefited from communicating "away from the polarizing spotlight [. . .] to build relationships of mutual respect and understanding; to help deescalate the rhetoric of the abortion controversy". Participants related that, "we would not interrupt, grandstand, or make personal attacks. We would speak for ourselves, not as representatives of organizations" (ibid.). This, rather non-partisan approach, transcends the traditional posturing found in adversarial models of communication and resulted in the participants speaking openly, listening to each other with care and respect and increasing their affection and understanding for one another. They concluded that this process, while not necessarily changing their views, helped them understand the value of dialogue in contributing "to a more civil and compassionate society" (Bone et al., 2008:454).

This freedom and "power to choose or decide" forms the last condition of invitational rhetoric (Foss & Griffin, 1997:12) and is also applicable to deliberation culture. It emerged in the second case study referred to in Chapter 3, where talk show guests were not handed a packaged conclusion but were rather invited to decide for themselves when the right time to marry would be or what the implications of teenage pregnancy might be. This freedom to suspend judgment, to reflect and probe, echoes *pungwe*, the traditional, *ubuntu*-based approach to discourse where communities get together to consult on any and all matters and explore solutions collectively even should this take a long time and require a great effort (see Blankenberg, 1999:46).

In summary, the rhetorical approach of deliberation culture is to engage in a respectful and equal exchange from which all parties walk away with an enriched understanding. This does not mean that persuasive exchanges cannot be respectful or that persuasion cannot also be present, but rather, that the main aim of communication can at times be to develop a more complete worldview rather than to relentlessly advocate the adoption of a specific stance.

Identity/Positioning

Worldviews also play a decisive role in determining a theoretical approach to identity in deliberation culture: "My humanity is caught up, is inextricably bound up in yours" (Tutu, 1999:31).

This *ubuntu* conception of identity was far from operational in the early 1990s in South Africa. For Nelson Mandela and all those who were vested in changing this, the task was to build a discursive community that included "all South Africans as an indispensable pre-condition to a common political community" (Mandela, 1994:197). Furthermore:

> This stood in contrast with the ideology of apartheid, which pretended that black South Africans were residents of fictitious 'homelands,' and also with the racialist assumptions of the Pan-Africanist Congress (among other groups) for whom white South Africans were no more than 'foreign minority groups' or 'aliens' with no natural place in South Africa.
>
> (ibid.)

In the context of developing an approach to communication rooted in *ubuntu*, the idea of identity espoused by its deeply relational understanding of power motivates an all-encompassing discursive community or an overarching 'we'. Related to this, Burke (1969) suggests that like-minded individuals often transcend or transform their differences and identify instead with a higher principle. The various facets of an individual or the various individuals on one side of an argument ascend from their original positions and become consubstantial with each other (Burke, 1969:19–27). Deliberation culture, however, extends this idea to include all participants of a communicative act without constructing another side/party/camp. Exhibiting deliberation culture in public discourse means cultivating diversity of thought while pursuing common ground. This emphasizes the idea of our common humanity while taking plurality very seriously (see Louw, 2001:21). So while my individuality constitutes a uniqueness, "My humanity is caught up, is inextricably bound up in yours" (Tutu, 1999:31; see also Mkhize, 2008:39–40; Mnyaka & Motlhabi, 2009:69).

This does not mean that differences are brushed over or ignored. On the contrary, differences can only emerge, be accepted and worked through from within the appreciation of a common humanity. As Louw (2010:4) suggests:

> Ubuntu dictates that, if we are to be human, we need to recognize the genuine otherness of our fellow citizens. That is, we need to acknowledge

the diversity of languages, histories, values and customs, all of which constitute [. . .] society.

At another time Louw (2001:21) proposes that while *ubuntu*, "constitutes personhood through other persons, it appreciates the fact that 'other persons' are so called, precisely because we can ultimately never quite 'stand in their shoes' or completely 'see through their eyes'". The premise is that, while we are each uniquely endowed with insights that no other participant may be able to offer, the I/other dichotomy is replaced with an appreciation of 'we' (Louw, 2010:16). In other words there is no need, as Burke (1969) suggests, for the construction of an oppositional identity. There is, however, a need for distinction and complementarity. *Ubuntu* incorporates dialogue through connectivity and distance. It holds dear the uniqueness of the other without estranging it from 'we' (see Kimmerle, 2006). Deliberation culture then, cultivates unity in diversity. Being an individual means being with others (Louw, 2010:15). This focuses deliberation in the direction of consensus, which is never forced but rather encouraged or nurtured (see Mandela, 1994:134). It also allows for each individual viewpoint to be fully appreciated in what becomes a harmonious blend of complementary clues to something that is bigger than the sum of its parts.

A deliberative model of public discourse rooted in *ubuntu*, then, expands the notion of 'we' identities to its widest possible sense. The notion of 'humanness' that underlies all theoretical work on *ubuntu* and which, some argue, extends to connectivity with all life on the planet and to other dimensions (see Bhengu, 1996:38), is particularly relevant in this regard. Its focus on our common humanity allows us to think and talk differently about our perceived interests and identities. And while I'm cognizant of the controversial tribal and historical processes of initiation that are associated with *ubuntu* (see Kimmerle, 1995; Ramose, 2002) and its sometimes ambiguous stance toward non-Africans (see Van Binsbergen, 2001), *ubuntu*'s normative interpretation makes space for a universality that emphasizes inclusiveness as individuality within interdependence. In this way, *ubuntu* has a trans-cultural character (Christians, 2004) and recognizes that "the role of community in making the world human" is not just African but a "universal order that conditions the nature of humans generally" (Wiredu, 2004:493). This evolves traditional discourses that have been confined by national, tribal, religious or other fragmented notions of identity. Such lesser notions of identity prevent societies from subordinating their short-term goals to the wellbeing of the greater human good. As long as nations identify as 'nations first' and view their interests as more valuable or defendable than those of others, they struggle to find sustainable solutions to shared environmental, economic or political challenges. However, progress is possible when our common humanity becomes an overarching identity and a "plurality of personalities" in a "multiplicity of relationships" (Louw, 2010:4) informs our reality.

Yet even if we assume, as some do (see Burke, 1969) that oppositional identity formation is necessary, this could

> [. . .] be constructed on the basis of difference from hypothetical values and the imagined collective identities centered on them, or on the basis of difference from the values of a past historical identity from which one wishes to mark one's distance [. . .] humanity's own past provides a rich and terrifying repository in contrast to which cosmopolitan identity could constitute its 'difference'.
>
> (Abizadeh, 2005:50–51)

An inclusive 'we' identity is enabling as it allows for the cultivation of diversity and fluidity without marginalizing texture and nuance. In the context of post-*apartheid* South Africa, for example, Salazar (2002:102) traces how self-definition went from the broad perceptions of 'White', 'Colored' and 'Black' to a remarkably fluid perception that ranged from " 'Cape Colored' to 'Tswana' but also from 'quite White' to 'African', from 'Boer' to 'Child of God', from 'English' to 'Afrikaaner' and often simply 'South African' ". According to him, people have "multiple, overlapping, non-exclusive and partial identities", which they base on ideas such as "gender, age, family, ethnicity, nationality, religious beliefs, occupation, personal interest, socio-economic status and so forth"—none of which inherently "preclude a sense of 'oneness' with others" (ibid.). This superseding sense of oneness or humanness is a prerequisite for deliberation culture and liberates multiplicity.

It also implies that communicators do not adhere too strongly to their transient categorizations or to their ensuing positions. Instead of holding unremittingly to personal views and positional statements they acknowledge instead the contingency and relativity of their views and experiences without relinquishing their value or validity. Individual truth is seen as somewhat relative and perspectives as complementary. The underlying epistemology is rooted in acknowledging the limitations of personal views and the illimitable power of the collective. Thus, as Christians (2004) proposes, the cultivation of diverse views is paramount in an *ubuntu* conception of the world. In considering unrealistic and unproductive the role of objectivity for journalists, Christians also calls for media practitioners and citizens to disclose their views and embed them historically and biographically. This implies self-reflexivity so that participants of a discourse conceive of their beliefs with some measure of distance (see Louw, 2001:21).

However, notions of objectivity need not be discarded entirely. It is very possible to conceive of a 'higher' truth, even if only conceptually, toward which citizens and media people can strive and which materializes the more people participate collectively.

Of course, as is the case with *ubuntu* more generally and with many other concepts, an expansive 'we' identity can and has been misappropriated, particularly in favor of White (male) privilege. Generalizing their experiences and values as the master narrative, Anglo-European wo/men have increasingly come under attack for sidelining and even silencing those of many others. While severely problematic, this corruption and misappropriation does not make the fundamental concept of a diversely constituted 'we' inherently abusive.

Mediation and Consensus

Beyond enabling a sense of 'we' and of collective progress on various matters for those engaged in deliberation culture, the producers, presenters and facilitators involved in its mediation "also have an obligation to present content that would [. . .] improve their quality of life" (Metz, 2015:83). In other words, the focus of a meeting, conference, think tank, political roundtable or talk show that exhibits deliberation culture would be in some way associated with the aim to serve the transformation of society (Wasserman & De Beer, 2005).

With that aim in mind, the facilitator in deliberation culture has an important role to play, but is not more important than other participants. She is a mediator that takes into account multiple interpretations and cultural complexities (see Duncan & Seloane, 1998). She opens up the widest possible set of interests and concerns (see Rodny-Gumede, 2015). Her role is to articulate the various facets of the issues at hand, taking care to adequately illicit the participation of as many voices as possible, particularly those less vocal. "The goal of the media or the mediator becomes identifying representative voices and communities rather than spectacular ones that are anecdotal and idiosyncratic" (Christians, 2004:249). These voices do not just include experts but particularly ordinary citizens from a wide range of socio-economic, racial, educational and experiential backgrounds. She becomes the 'gate-opener' rather than a 'gate-keeper' and looks "for ways in which [. . .] narratives are connected, interrelated and interdependent" (Wasserman, 2013:78). As a moderator, she encourages participants to listen and actively integrates perceived conflicts and dualities by reframing the contributions of those she engages with and drawing out their underlying motives. As Rothman (1997:171) proposes, "Moving from positional debating to real communication requires a lot of analysis of underlying motivations, hopes, fears", which more often than not integrate into similar overarching intentions. In her quest to uncover these intentions, the mediator also shifts the focus away from personal affronts and mudslinging exercises and toward a discussion of ethical issues. As was the case in the second case study mentioned in Chapter 3, those engaged in a discourse can discuss the validity or appropriateness of actions, approaches and strategies without personally attacking the people who employ them. It is only in this way that the media can become a catalyst for moral agency and rise above spectacle (see Christians, 2004:248).

Contrary to what we see so often today, where personal attacks and hurtful caricatures appear harmless if not necessary, *ubuntu* cultivates communication with a higher purpose. It strives for consensus, cohesion and mutual exposure in dialogue. Its central premise is participation as an element of connection, which includes those who may appear at first difficult to relate to. Thus, the facilitator also maintains dignity and civility as she deals with any breaches to the general harmony and exhibits discord and authority to the extent necessary to restore justice (see Chasi, 2014b; Metz, 2015). Should a communicator exhibit ill will or injustice, for example in the form of a racist or personally threatening statement, she can remove that person from the forum until such time as she or he commits to the principles of deliberation culture. So while in charge of cultivating and maintaining the framework for deliberation culture, the mediator is also part of the bigger 'we' and engages in "a process of learning as both 'facilitator' and 'participant'" (Blankenberg, 1999:46). Her own views are very much encouraged when appropriately contextualized and her mediation occurs in a "facilitatory manner" that is "consultative and ongoing" (Blankenberg, 1999:45). Her role is not that of a watchdog, but of someone who strives for consensus, much like a negotiator (Fourie, 2011:38). Coming back to my musical analogy, she is, in some ways, the conductor, setting the pace, accentuating, encouraging, restraining the deliberation and looking to illicit the bigger symphony for all to experience.

In this context, Nelson Mandela (1994:18–19) describes the role of a tribal regent in bringing the bigger picture into clearer focus:

> His purpose was to sum up what had been said and form some consensus among the diverse opinions. But no conclusion was forced on people who disagreed. If no agreement could be reached, another meeting would be held.

Mandela (1994) and Blankenberg (1999) describe such community meetings as continuing until some kind of consensus was reached. These consultative gatherings usually resulted in unanimity or not at all: "Unanimity, however, might be an agreement to disagree, to wait for a more propitious time to propose a solution. Democracy meant all men were to be heard, and a decision was taken together as a people" (Mandela, 1994:19). In deliberation culture, then, all wo/men are to be heard and consensus is a desirable goal, nurtured through the creative work of a facilitator.

From within the realism of *ubuntu*, which fashions an organic worldview of harmony and cohesion and operates from the premise that human nature is profoundly relational and other-oriented, collective decision-making can be seen as the most appropriate strategy for social progress because consensus in this context means "open-endedness, contingency and flux" (Louw, 2001:26). Human interests are seen as bound-up and consensus becomes an expression of mutual empowerment by the collective: "Not only is unanimous decision-making constitutive of shared identity, it is likely to promote both shared identity and good-will in the long run more than majoritarianism since the minority would feel less excluded from the political process" (Metz, 2007:339). Participatory decision-making enables every person to speak up until, in the widest sense, "some kind of an agreement, consensus or group cohesion is reached" (Louw, 2001:19).

This harmonious collaboration, be it of diverse and differing opinions, is reflected in words like *simunye*, which means 'we are one' or 'unity is strength' (Broodryk, 1997:5). By fostering a 'we' identity, coordinating behavior and realizing shared ends (see Metz, 2014b:6763), consultative deliberation fulfills the "requirement to produce harmony and to reduce discord" (Metz, 2007:340). This process is not marked by a pressure to agree, but rather a 'desire' to agree (Louw, 2001:19) and is there "to safeguard the rights and opinions of individuals and minorities". This principle is applied in *lekgotla*, which broadly means 'meeting circle' or 'tribal management' and where a council sits in deliberation and all voices are heard (De Liefde,

2005). *Lekgotla* is also informed by *ubuntu* and its principles of group deci-sion-making have been applied to mutualistic management theories (see ibid.). In *ubuntu* and *lekgotla*, participants of a discourse agree to disagree (Louw, 2010) when consensus cannot be found.

This process is not to "be confused with outmoded and suspect crav-ings for an oppressive universal hegemonic sameness" (ibid.:4; see also Ramose, 2002:105–106; Van der Merwe, 1996:12). Agreeing to disagree means that the minority's "constructive input is still acknowledged or rec-ognized in communal decisions" (Louw, 2001:21) as the preservation of relations or unity are deemed more valuable than adherence to personal views or economic and material wellbeing (Metz, 2009). However, a "will-ingness to compromise" is reached and a way forward is articulated with a "voluntary acquiescence of the momentary minority" (Wiredu, 1998:380). Such a voluntary acquiescence helps community members to "come to a [. . .] quick decision and to follow a particular course of action" (Louw, 2010:4) in the interest of generating momentum. This concerted and col-lective action toward a common goal can be reconsidered should it prove ineffective in reaching its original goals. This may be what Bhengu (1996) refers to as the essence of democracy, which enables a path beyond left or right, black or white, pro and con and toward a diverse and deeply relational discursive community.

In summary then, deliberation culture offers an open-ended, integrative approach to framing, where authentic disclosure is provided and diversity is appreciated and encouraged. Communicators take a chiefly exploratory posture that is aimed at increasing understanding and reaching consensus. Identity is constructed in terms of a broader and diversely constituted 'we', where there is a level of distance from one's position and mediation occurs in a consultative, unifying and facilitatory manner. This approach to public discourse is not merely theoretical but emerges practically at various times, in various settings and through its various facets. My project here has been to formalize it as a coherent concept and to bring attention to it so that inno-vations may occur in the theory and practice of discourse and communica-tion. In the concluding chapter I now consider what limitations may hinder its application and what settings could benefit from it.

References

Abizadeh, A. (2005). Does Collective Identity Presuppose an Other? On the Alleged Incoherence of Global Solidarity. *American Political Science Review*, 99(1): 45–60.

Bahá'í International Community (1995). The Prosperity of Humankind, Statement presented at the United Nations World Summit on Social Development, 3 March 1995, Copenhagen, Denmark.

Bhengu, M.J. (1996). *Ubuntu: The Essence of Democracy*. Cape Town: Novalis.

Bickford, S. (1996). *The Dissonance of Democracy: Listening, Conflict and Citizenship*. Ithaca: Cornell University Press.

Blankenberg, N. (1999). In Search of Real Freedom: Ubuntu and the Media. *Critical Arts*, 12(2):42–65.

Bone, J.E., Griffin, C.L. & Scholz, T.L.M. (2008). Beyond Traditional Conceptualizations of Rhetoric: Invitational Rhetoric and a Movement toward Civility. *Western Journal of Communication*, 72(4):434–462.

Briand, M. (1995). *Building Deliberative Communities*. Charlottesville: Pew Partnerships for Civic Change.

Bridges, D. (1994). Deliberation and Decision Making. In Dillon, J.T. (ed). *Deliberation in Education and Society*: 67–80, Norwood: Ablex Publishing Corporation.

Broodryk, J. (1997). Ubuntuism as a Worldview to Order Society, Doctoral Dissertation, Pretoria: University of South Africa.

Burke, K. (1969). *A Rhetoric of Motives*. Berkeley: University of California Press.

Chasi, C. (2014a). Ubuntu and Freedom of Expression. *Ethics & Behavior*, 24(6): 495–509.

Chasi, C. (2014b). Violent Communication Is Not Alien to Ubuntu: Nothing Human Is Alien to Africans. *Communicatio: South African Journal for Communication Theory and Research*, 40(4):287–304.

Christians, C.G. (2004). Ubuntu and Communitarianism in Media Ethics. *Ecquid Novi*, 25(2):235–256.

Couldry, N. (2010). *Why Voice Matters: Culture and Politics after Neoliberalism*. London: Sage.

De Liefde, W.H.J. (2005). *Lekgotla: The Art of Leadership through Dialogue*. Cape Town: Jacana.

Denzin, N. (1997). *Interpretive Ethnography: Ethnographic Practices of the 21st Century*. Thousand Oaks: Sage.

Derrida, J. (1967). *Of Grammatology*. Baltimore: Johns Hopkins University Press.

Deutsch, M. (2000). Cooperation and Competition. In Deutsch, M. & Coleman, P. (eds). *The Handbook of Conflict Resolution: Theory and Practice*: 21–40, San Francisco: Jossey-Bass.

Dillon, J.T. (1994). *Deliberation in Education and Society*. Norwood: Ablex Publishing Corporation.

Duncan, J. & Seloane, M. (1998). Introduction. In Duncan, J. & Seloane, M. (eds). *Media and Democracy in South Africa*: 1–53, Pretoria: HSRC.

Emmet, D. (2009). The Concept of Power. In Champlin, J. (ed). *Paradigms of Political Power*: 78–106, New Brunswick, NJ: Transaction Publishers.

Fairclough, N. (2003). *Analyzing Discourse: Textual Analysis for Social Research*. London: Routledge.

Foss, S. & Griffin, C. (1997). Transforming Rhetoric through Feminist Reconstruction: A Response to the Gender Diversity Perspective. *Women's Studies in Communication*, 20(2):117–135.

Fourie, P. (2011). Normative Media Theory in a Changed Media Landscape and Globalized Society. In Hyde-Clarke, N. (ed). *Communication and Media Ethics in South Africa*: 25–45, Cape Town: Juta.

Galtung, J. (2004). *Transcend and Transform*. London: Pluto.

Gilligan, C. (1993). *In a Different Voice: Psychological Theory and Women's Development*. Cambridge: Harvard University Press.

Karlberg, M. (2004). *Beyond the Culture of Contest*. Oxford: George Ronald.

Kelly, R. (2013). The Binary Problem: Marginalizing Important Issues Related to Gun Violence, Paper presented at the University of Arizona, 2 April 2013, Phoenix, USA.

Kimmerle, H. (2006). Ubuntu and Communalism in African Philosophy and Art. In Van den Heuvel, H., Mangaliso, M. & Van de Bunt, L. (eds). *Prophecies and Protest: Ubuntu in Global Management*. Cape Town: Unisa Press.

Kolstoe, J.E. (1990). *Consultation: A Universal Lamp of Guidance*. Oxford: George Ronald.

Louw, D.J. (2001). Ubuntu and the Challenge of Multiculturalism in Post-Apartheid South Africa, Unitwin Student Network, www.phys.uu.nl/~unitwin/, Accessed 4 November 2014.

Louw, D.J. (2010). Power Sharing and the Challenge of Ubuntu Ethics, Paper presented at the Forum for Religious Dialogue Symposium of the Research Institute for Theology and Religion at the University of South Africa, January 2010, Pretoria, South Africa.

Mandela, N. (1994). *Long Walk to Freedom: The Autobiography of Nelson Mandela*. Boston: Little Brown.

Masolo, D.A. (2010). *Self and Community in a Changing World*. Bloomington: Indiana University Press.

Metz. T. (2007). Toward an African Moral Theory. *Journal of Political Philosophy*, 15(1):321–341.

Metz, T. (2009). African Moral Theory and Public Governance: Nepotism, Preferential Hiring and Other Partiality. In Munyaradzi, F.M. (ed). *African Ethics: An Anthology for Comparative and Applied Ethics*: 335–356, Pietermaritzburg: University of KwaZulu-Natal Press.

Metz, T. (2011). Ubuntu as a Moral Theory and Human Rights in South Africa. *African Human Rights Law Journal*, 11(1):532–559.

Metz, T. (2014a). Harmonizing Global Ethics in the Future: A Proposal to Add South and East to West. *Journal of Global Ethics*, 10(2):146–155.

Metz, T. (2014b). Ubuntu: The Good Life. In Michalos, A. (ed). *Encyclopedia of Quality of Life and Well-Being Research*. Dordrecht: Springer.

Metz, T. (2015). African Ethics and Journalism Ethics: News and Opinion in Light of Ubuntu. *Journal of Media Ethics: Exploring Questions of Media Morality*, 30(2):74–90.

Metz, T. & Gaie, J. (2010). The African Ethic of Ubuntu/Botho: Implications for Research on Morality. *Journal of Moral Education*, 39(1):273–290.

Mkhize, N. (2008). Ubuntu and Harmony: An African Approach to Morality and Ethics. In Nicolson, R. (ed). *Persons in Community: African Ethics in a Global Culture*: 35–44, Pietermaritzburg: University of KwaZulu-Natal Press.

Mnyaka, M. & Motlhabi, M. (2005). The African Concept of Ubuntu/Botho and Its Socio-Moral Significance. *Black Theology*, 3(1):215–237.

Mnyaka, M. & Motlhabi, M. (2009). Ubuntu and Its Socio-Moral Significance. In Murove, M.F. (ed). *African Ethics: An Anthology of Comparative and Applied Ethics*: 63–84, Pietermaritzburg: University of KwaZulu-Natal Press.

Moriarty, T.A. (2003). *Finding the Words: A Rhetorical History of South Africa's Transition from Apartheid to Democracy*. London: Praeger.

Noah, T. (2015). *The Daily Show*, 30 September 2015.

Ramose, M.B. (2002/1999). *African Philosophy through Ubuntu*. Harare: Mond Books.

Rodny-Gumede, Y. (2015). An Assessment of the Public Interest and Ideas of the Public in South Africa and the Adoption of Ubuntu Journalism. *Journal of Mass Media Ethics*, 30(2):109–124.

Rothman, J. (1997). *Resolving Identity-Based Conflicts in Nations, Organizations and Communities*. San Francisco: Jossey-Bass.

Salazar, P.J. (2002). *An African Athens: Rhetoric and the Shaping of Democracy in South Africa*. Mahwah: Lawrence Erlbaum.

Shutte, A. (2001). *Ubuntu: An Ethic for the New South Africa*. Cape Town: Cluster Publications.

Tankard, J.W., Hendrickson, L., Silberman, J., Bliss, K. & Chanem, S. (1991). Media Frames: Approaches to Conceptualization and Measurement, Paper presented at the Association for Education in Journalism and Mass Communication Annual Meeting, August 1991, Boston, USA.

Tannen, D. (1998). *The Argument Culture*. New York: Random House.

Tutu, D. (1999). *No Future without Forgiveness*. New York: Random House.

Van Binsbergen, W. (2001). Ubuntu and the Globalization of Southern African Thought and Society. *Quest: An African Journal of Philosophy*, 15(1–2):53–89.

Van der Merwe, M.L. (1996). Philosophy and the Multi-Cultural Context of (Post) apartheid South Africa. *Ethical Perspectives*, 3(2):1–15.

Wasserman, H. (2013). Journalism in a New Democracy: The Ethics of Listening. *Communicatio: South African Journal for Communication Theory and Research*, 39(1):67–84.

Wasserman, H. & De Beer, A.S. (2005). Which Public? Whose Interest? The South African Media and Its Role During the First Ten Years of Democracy. *Critical Arts*, 19(1–2): 36–51.

Wiredu, K. (1998). Democracy and Consensus in African Traditional Politics: A Plea for a Non-Party Polity. In Coetzee, P.H. & Roux, A.P.J. (eds). *Philosophy from Africa*: 374–382, Johannesburg: International Thomson.

5   Conclusion

I began this project by discussing some principle theories around discourse, culture and power. I outlined some prevalent ways in which discourses pan out and how they are mostly shaped by normative values inherited from the global North. In particular, I presented 'argument culture' (Tannen, 1998) as a widely occurring phenomenon. I proposed that it can be both valuable and potentially limiting in many contexts where collaboration is possible and very much desirable. I also introduced the African philosophy of *ubuntu* as a normative framework, which could ground a deeply relational and collaborative approach to public discourse. I termed this approach 'deliberation culture' and teased out some of its objectives, principles and elements. In this final chapter, I now discuss how deliberation culture relates to some other models of communication, what its possible applications could be and what conditions are necessary for it to thrive.

Derived from harmonious, cohesive and relational understandings of power and human relations, deliberation culture is a communal and collaborative form of inquiry, which encourages the contextualization and flexibility of views and which stimulates diversity and participation. Deliberation culture is both dialogical and deliberative in its objectives and exhibits and cultivates an open-ended approach to framing; an invitational and exploratory form of rhetoric; an all-encompassing 'we' identity and a facilitatory type of mediation. What distinguishes it from many other models of public discourse are its deeper assumptions around human nature and social relations, which derive from the African moral theory of *ubuntu*.

Abrahamson's (2004) idea of 'confrontative dialogue', for example, is one model that exhibits similar aims yet evidences a fundamentally different premise. The overarching aim of confrontative dialogue is to actively cultivate a discursive community where deep conflict is bridged. Much like in deliberation culture, communicators are encouraged not to hold on too firmly to their views. Likewise, winning an argument is not the aim of the exercise. Rather, the aim is to "transcend and transform" patterns of thought, to "visualize divergences and differences" and to make an effort to "sympathize with the motives and logic" of the other (Abrahamson, 2004:4). In this way confrontative dialogue employs a rather invitational and exploratory stance and is highly participatory. Yet the differences and coinciding interests it explores are probed with a view to strengthening the leverage of disenfranchised parties (ibid.), which suggests that these mutualistic aims are not necessarily premised on relationality. Rather, in confrontative dialogue, the underlying understanding of power is conflictual. In particular, it assumes sides, camps and parties with oppositional interests and suggests that the best way forward is to balance or leverage these interests. The process of articulating interests and voicing possible positions is therefore designed to strengthen the identity and legitimacy of the weaker party.

In deliberation culture, on the other hand, the articulation of those interests and positions contributes to and is informed by a larger 'we' identity among its participants. In this way, deliberation culture loosens positions and positional statements while confrontative dialogue may entrench them by strengthening the 'weaker' side. In this process, confrontative dialogue becomes somewhat "threatening to elites" because the more efficient it is "for the powerless and weaker partner, the more difficult" it becomes "to get the more powerful and stronger partner to participate" (Abrahamson, 2004:8). In deliberation culture, on the other hand, where interests are presumed to be enmeshed and complementary, all participants remain equally vested in the process. The concept of an elite falls away altogether as power is conceived of in terms of a deeply relational force. Those with more material resources see themselves as profoundly bound-up with those who have less.

These differing conceptions underlying each approach lead one model to embrace consensus-driven deliberation and the other to shy away from it—both with the very legitimate aim of cultivating diversity and social justice. In his experience of working in international development cooperation specifically, Abrahamson frequently witnesses the misappropriation of consensus:

> At times, peace agreements are short-lived as they do not tackle the proper roots of conflict [. . .] or are not negotiated by parties sufficiently legitimate within society in order for the agreement to be implemented and respected. In the same way various agreements on international

development cooperation do not always include needs and require-
ments of the recipient country but reflect only conditionalities imposed
by the donors.

(Abrahamson, 2004:5)

Operating from within the prevalent realism of contemporary politics and
diplomacy, and with Gramsci's idea of a 'war of positions' as its point of
departure (see ibid.), Abrahamson's model effectively confronts the ensuing injustices and power inequalities. It creates an "improved understanding between partners whose relationship is asymmetric and characterized
by important conceptual gaps and strong mistrust" (Abrahamson, 2004:1).
As such, the model is designed for asymmetric relations, where the gap
between the powerless and the powerful is conceptualized as being sub-
stantial. The related aim "is to make visible the diverging values and interests behind the different formulations of the problems and measures to be
taken that the decision makers and their opponents have proposed" (Abrahamson, 2004:7). This implies that divergent interests can, at best, lead to
a redistribution of power in somewhat more equitable ways. In deliberation culture on the other hand, which assumes profound interrelatedness,
consensus becomes enabling rather than oppressive and is instrumental for
social progress. It ensures that everyone is incorporated in the process of
decision-making and is equally vested in ensuring the success (rather than
the sabotage) of whatever plans have been actioned.

While confrontative dialogue is arguably the more 'realistic' model of
discourse in a world deeply shaped by 'normative adversarialism' (see
Karlberg, 2004), it need not be the only option. If, as is the prerequisite of
deliberation culture, stakeholders are willing to operate from within a realism that espouses profoundly relational and immaterial understandings of
power, they can pursue options that further a wider array of complementary
goals and interests and which can benefit society at large. Deliberation culture, therefore, requires a genuine willingness to participate, a desire to step
back and listen and a readiness to step outside of what we have collectively
accepted as the nature of things.

Yet that willingness may not always be a given. As Ramsbotham (2010:134)
asks, "what if you do want to fight or are seeking public vindication or are
just too angry to meet?" Taking a moment to consider this scenario helps
contextualize deliberation culture further and determines when it does and
does not hold value for public discourse. Ramsbotham (2010:79) brings up
the compelling example of holocaust denial in parts of Europe and across

the Middle East, saying that it would be difficult if not impossible for him
to consider a point of view that denies its existence:

> So far as I am concerned to 'understand' why some people believe such
> patent untruths is to imply to find explanations for why the other holds
> such false beliefs. For me to pretend otherwise in this case would be a
> shame.

According to Ramsbotham (2010), radical disagreement stems from intractable conflict in which attempts at settlement and transformation have so far
failed. Radical disagreement manifests as strongly agonistic dialogue and is
in some ways the antithesis of deliberation culture. It involves a deep conflict of belief on how we should live and a profound clash of perspectives,
horizons and visual fields. Radical disagreement is located at the intersec-
tion of human difference, human discourse and human conflict (Ramsbotham, 2010:16):

> In radical disagreement the challenger does not vacate public space in
> response or try to resist only from the margins or attempt to transfer the
> struggle to a new discursive arena supposedly free from domination
> or even want to share the public space with the hegemonic discourse.

As with the case of Israel and Palestine, Ramsbotham (2010:16) suggests
that radical disagreement occurs when conflict parties recommend incompatible outcomes, there is a clash of discourses and each narrative seeks to
occupy the whole discursive space. Therefore, a radical disagreement is a
singularity rather than a plurality in the universe of discourse. The underlying notion of power is one of absolute domination. "In asymmetric conflicts the challenging discourse is the discourse of the materially weaker
party [. . .] in terms of control, of territory, military capacity and economic
resources" (Ramsbotham, 2010:170) but the aim of the challenger is also to
occupy the whole narrative and eliminate the other even if it risks its own
annihilation. "Radical disagreement is about what it is about" (Ramsbotham, 2010:125). In other words, it is not about the possibility of competing
narratives or abstract conceptualizations of discourse. Rather, participants
are fully identified with their positions, completely persuasive in their
approach and will not accept a reality or outcome other than their own,
which is irrefutably 'true'. "This is not a coexistence of rival discourses, but
a fight to the death to impose the one discourse" (ibid.).

This need to impose one's truth on another further differentiates radical disagreement from deliberation culture. While deliberation culture does not inherently or categorically exclude the possibility of an overarching truth or the possibility of people finding or retaining a universal/foundational truth they feel is valid, its participants are not vested in imposing this on others. They are amenable to exploration, to a search for common ground and to the possibility of agreeing to disagree. In radical disagreement, on the other hand, conflict parties refuse to separate positions from interests and needs, refuse to reframe competition into shared problem-solving, are not willing to transform adversarial debate into constructive dialogue, will not change statements into questions and do not fuse horizons (see Ramsbotham, 2010). They fail to recognize the systemic nature of conflict or that they may only have a partial view of it and they do not acknowledge that the other's narrative or experience may be legitimate. Communicators do not recognize overlapping interests and are not prepared to transform the language and practice of power into an ideal speech situation (ibid.:166).

According to Ramsbotham, in these cases there can be no conflict resolution. Instead of transforming or even bypassing the radical disagreement, he suggests it needs to be embraced more fully. In other words, there needs to be more conflict before social change can occur. The idea is to intensify the conflict and to turn up the heat as it were. "In highly complex conflict systems experience suggests that it is when the outlook seems bleakest that possibilities for change can unexpectedly open up and 'hard-liners' can sometimes deliver change more easily than 'moderates'" (Ramsbotham, 2010:169). When the process is successful conflict parties otherwise not amenable to transformative communication are brought to a point where they may have an incentive to participate in constructive communication. Similarly, in the above-mentioned model of confrontative dialogue, the tipping point arrives "when contradictions in the system become unmanageable and are conceived by dominant elite groups to [be] threaten[ing] their own long-term security interests" (Abrahamson, 2004:3). In other words, change occurs when all parties recognize, or are forced to recognize, the variable-sum nature of their goals. This is where deliberation culture becomes effective and advantageous.

As such deliberation culture, confrontative dialogue and radical disagreement each fulfill a unique role and occupy a time and place of maximum efficacy. The same is true for argument culture. In a reality program where participants pitch their business ideas to investors, for example, it may be very useful for those investors to employ some level of persuasion and argumentation in challenging the business plans presented to them. In this way they can prevent their protégés from making fatal mistakes with their money down the line. Deliberation culture, then, is a mutualistic alternative to argument culture that is desirable where collaboration is advantageous and which becomes operational 'before' radical disagreement and 'after' radical disagreement (and confrontative dialogue). It posits that underneath adversarial positions and clashing values, there exist some shared basic human needs. Once participants of a discourse identify with these needs, the sole occupation of the discourse, of the 'territory', or of 'Jerusalem' (see Ramsbotham, 2010:8) becomes less significant and conflict can be resolved. Because of this, deliberation culture may be a relevant and effective strategy for social change in many areas where disagreement ceases to be radical and people are genuinely vested in letting go and moving forward.

In order to do so, Venables (2016:2) suggests that we transcend our prevalent social strategies, which continue to cause "prolonged economic stagnation, widespread environmental degradation, rising extremism, increased militarization and the displacement of millions of people" and that we search instead for a path where change is "harnessed to lead us gently down to a more materially modest, more stable, more equitable form of social and economic organization". In this process, post-colonial/post-conflict societies such as South Africa play a significant role as they offer evolving notions of social change based in reconciliation, collaboration and *ubuntu*. These are values that stand in contrast to the normative frameworks of liberal democracy that are so often applied across the globe and that, as Venables suggests, are failing to address the very needs of our globe.

The significance of the idea of *ubuntu* in modern societies, then, may not so much be to revolutionize or bring back lost values but rather to work with and evolve society in a forward looking manner. This process is ongoing. As such, the idea of deliberation culture is open to further contemplation, experimentation and reflection. It presents one of many ways in which we can rethink how we relate as human beings and how we can communicate, organize and advance as societies that share a graciously abundant planet. Through the lens of *ubuntu* our perspective changes. 'Development' discourses can be re-conceptualized in terms of the freedom to enter more deeply into community with others rather than as an instrument for advancing the interests of global capitalism and reproducing the same hierarchy of power of nations. From within its realism, 'progress' is,

> underscored by ethical and ecological reciprocity and responsibility to another and is 'for' the globe's eco-systems within which humanity finds

mutualism rather than at the their expense, or rather, anthropomorphic-
ally, at the expense of the environment in favor of a select group.

(Swanson, 2012:30)

In this context it is vital to experiment practically with deliberation culture
and to explore how *ubuntu* and its approach to communication might relate
to other, similarly cohesive and harmonious models of communication, for
example to the Bahá'í idea of 'consultation' (see Kolstoe, 1990), and how
these forms of discourse can be applied in various settings such as in economics, governance or in legal and educational contexts.

In education, for example, deliberative and consultative models of communication could enhance classroom learning as students explore a subject
in participatory rather than uni-directional ways and teachers assume or
assign the role of facilitator. This could contribute to de-colonizing efforts
that reshape curricula not only in terms of their content but importantly in
terms of their de-centralized, participatory and *ubuntu*-based processes.

The field of economics and business could likewise benefit from mind-
set shifts. Competitive approaches and market principles could be comple-
mented with cooperative initiatives and strategies such as those exhibited
in South Africa's savings cooperatives or *stokvels*. In this context Abedian
(2015) suggests that even broader cooperations between the business sector and various other strata of society would also go a long way in solving
many seemingly intractable problems. He specifically highlights the case of
South Africa, where a breakdown in communication between the business
community and government has led to an impasse:

The adversarial attitude of those in power has sidelined a key stake-
holder, namely the business community. A different and more collaborative approach would draw on the capabilities of the business
sector to solve some of the urban management challenges facing this
country.

(ibid.:n.p.)

In the realm of governance, then, politicians, business leaders and civil society could come together to transcend their immediate agendas and to work
out sustainable and mutualistic solutions that are likely to benefit society as
a whole. In this scenario, public fora would become spaces where policy
makers, researchers and specialists; commentators, stakeholders and citizens could explore the causal forces of various issues in collaborative ways

and where they could interact with one another rather than against each other for the purpose of advancing collective goals.

In legal and judicial settings too, methodologies could be considered that harness the collective and exploratory pursuit of 'truth/justice' rather than the channeling of energies in adversarial ways. Instead of cultivating battles between the richest parties who have the craftiest lawyers, legal professionals, advocates and judges could see themselves as collaborators of one and the same side, investigating the fullest picture and considering the fairest judgments without being rewarded for a particular outcome and without having a vested interest in promoting, obscuring or distorting any facts.

And of course in the field of media and journalism a more representative approach would be conducive to deepening democracy, where journalists saw themselves as gate-openers and members of the community-at-large. In radio, television and the online space specific formats and set-ups could be designed and researched that exhibit deliberation culture and adapt it to suit the time-frame, setting and objective of a particular program. In view of the many commercial pressures that drive contemporary programming choices and impede innovations along mutualistic lines, the efficacy of deliberation culture and its audience receptivity would form specific points of interest and ways of drawing out engagement could be explored.

For all of these areas to benefit from a relational approach to discourse and communication and for a model like deliberation culture to reach its full potential, societies have to consciously and unconsciously operate from within a more naturalized framework such as that suggested by *ubuntu* or any other harmonious worldview. Without transforming our attitudes and perceptions, these structural changes remain utopian, idealistic and futile. Likewise, in order to cultivate and nurture alternative values and normative assumptions, it is important that we have exposure to different styles and strategies of social organization, that we experiment with more than the usual formats and programs, that we consider harmonious ways of relating and that we remain patient and open-minded as we evolve and grow. For this to happen creativity is called for. "As creators, distributors and users of culture, humans live in a world of their own making" (Christians, 2004:240). So recovering and refashioning discourses in ways that help amplify our deep human connectivity is not only an attractive challenge but also a real possibility and may help us flourish, if we only chose to explore this.

A notion of "humble togetherness" (Swanson, 2012:40) or *ubuntu* in facing the many challenges that beset our world can go a long way in providing alternatives to the way governments act in response to their perceived need to protect their own interests. It isn't until we recognize that our social, political and environmental concerns are interrelated that mutualistic paradigms in general and *ubuntu* specifically can begin to make a difference. Such a recognition goes hand in hand with the need to produce structural changes within democratic institutions. It also helps us with our daily, local and lived experiences. It allows us to reflect on and critically engage with these in less objectifying ways and enables us to understand our role in creating and overcoming the shared challenges we face as communities and societies. It offers hope and possibility by reshaping constructed meanings, identities and worldviews and by co-constructing alternatives that build on the collective strength of our diversity. *Ubuntu* as a form of social democratic engagement provides us with an opportunity for renewal and transformation, cooperation and mutual understanding in our quest to build a sustainable future for all the world's inhabitants.

Of course, for those with a cultural proximity to *ubuntu*, such intuitions may seem to come easier than for others but they still constitute a process. Many African people live in conditions similar to those under which the proverb emerged and many do not (see Suttner, 2017). As *ubuntu* suggests, personhood and relationality are not a given. Rather, they are to be achieved (see Ramose, 2002:65–66). Hence *ubuntu* is a lifelong process of becoming and relating, of striving and aspiring and one that we can embark on no matter where we come from. It finds its finest expression in the "non-discursive, non-argumentative, non-rational and subconscious spaces" (Louw, 2001:22) of society rather than in the realm of academia. *Ubuntu* and its manifestations of caring and sharing, of reconciliation and love are felt throughout the continent, "though you will probably not read about [it] in the papers or see [it] on cable news" (Louw, 2001:27).

With this book I hope to have shone a spotlight on this value, to have contributed to a synthesis of its many facets that are at once inclusive yet also emancipatory and to have stimulated thought and action in relation to its normative dimensions. I also hope to have advanced its understanding as an African philosophy while recognizing that its meanings are contested and that it exists alongside other, sometimes non-relational attitudes in the greater African context. I have advocated for *ubuntu* in providing legitimizing spaces for the transcendence of adversarialism and a more inclusive and fruitful engagement of human beings in relationship with one another and the world. As with any aspect of culture, *ubuntu* does not exist in stasis and evolves as it is spoken of and as it speaks to elements 'outside' of it. The harmonious, cohesive and relational understandings of life it engenders engage with and can be found in many of the world's ethical, religious, cultural and philosophical texts. They are not foreign or alien to our broader human experience and they emerge time and again, reminding us, as the famous Persian poet, Rumi (1207–1273), does, that:

> The words we speak become the house we live in. Speak a new language and the world will be a new world.

References

Abedian, I. (2015). Interview with author, Johannesburg, 18 February 2015.

Abrahamson, H. (2004). The Role of Dialogue in Confronting Power, Paper presented to the Department of Peace and Development Studies, January 2004, Gothenburg, Sweden.

Christians, C.G. (2004). Ubuntu and Communitarianism in Media Ethics. *Ecquid Novi*, 25(2):235–256.

Karlberg, M. (2004). *Beyond the Culture of Contest*. Oxford: George Ronald.

Kolstoe, J.E. (1990). *Consultation: A Universal Lamp of Guidance*. Oxford: George Ronald.

Louw, D.J. (2001). Ubuntu and the Challenge of Multiculturalism in Post-Apartheid South Africa, Unitwin Student Network, www.phys.uu.nl/~unitwin/, Accessed 4 November 2014.

Ramose, M. (2002). *African Philosophy through Ubuntu*. Harare: Rev ed Mond Books.

Ramsbotham, O. (2010). *Transforming Violent Conflict: Radical Disagreement, Dialogue and Survival*. London: Routledge.

Suttner, R. (2017). Op-Ed: Decolonising Project—What Is the Place of Ubuntu? *Daily Maverick*, 27 September, 2017, www.dailymaverick.co.za/article/2017-09-27-op-ed-decolonising-project-what-is-the-place-of-ubuntu/#.WcuJJkyB2YV, Accessed 27 September 2017.

Swanson, D.M. (2012). Ubuntu, African Epistemology and Development: Contributions, Tensions, Contradictions and Possibilities. In Wright, H.K. & Abdi, A.A. (eds). *The Dialectics of African Education and Western Discourses: Appropriation, Ambivalence and Alternatives*: 27–52, New York: Peter Lang.

Tannen, D. (1998). *The Argument Culture*. New York: Random House.

Venables, H. (2016). Things Are Going to Get Worse before They Get Worse. *Daily Maverick*, www.dailymaverick.co.za/opinionista/2016-01-14-things-are-going-to-get-worse-before-they-get-worse/?utm_, Accessed 14 January 2016.

Index

For Product Safety Concerns and Information please contact our
EU representative GPSR@taylorandfrancis.com Taylor & Francis
Verlag GmbH, Kaufingerstraße 24, 80331 München, Germany